Keep Calm and Carry On Complaining

How to Take On The Big Guys – and WIN!

by Duncan Peberdy

www.keepcalmbook.co.uk

First Edition published in the United Kingdom on 1st September 2020 by
DroitwichNet Limited
10 Mosel Drive - Droitwich Spa - Worcestershire - WR9 8DB

The right of Duncan Peberdy to be identified as the author of this work has been asserted in accordance with the Copyright, Designs and Patents Act 1988.

All rights reserved. No part of this publication may be reproduced, stored in a retrieval system, or transmitted in any form by any means electronic, mechanical, photocopying, recording or otherwise, without the prior written permission of the copyright owner.

A CIP record for this book is available from the British Library

The author and publisher have used their best efforts in preparing this book and disclaim liability rising directly or indirectly from the use and application of this book. If professional advice or other expert assistance is required, the services of a competent professional should be sought.

All reasonable efforts have been made to obtain necessary copyright permissions. Any omissions or errors are unintentional and will, if brought to the attention of the publisher, be corrected in future printings.

All brand names and product names found in this book are trade names, service makes, trademarks or registered trademarks of their respective owners, and used only for identification and explanation, without any intent to infringe.

ISBN: 978-0-9927903-3-2

Copyright © Duncan Peberdy 2020

Printed in the UK by Penrose Group
Units 7 & 8, Ashford Business Complex
Feltham Road, Ashford, TW15 1YQ
www.penrosegroup.co.uk

Table of Contents

Introduction	Page	5
Why Do I Complain?	Page	13
Experience 1 My BMW Experience	Page	19
Experience 2 TUI's Broken Sensatori Promise	Page	37
Experience 3 The Gateaux from the Chateau	Page	65
Experience 4 Would YOU buy a Volkswagen Tiguan?	Page	77
Experience 5 Getting Microsoft to "scratch beneath the Surface"	Page	93
Chapter 6 How to make sure that your Emails get read	Page	103
Chapter 7 Let's Build a Website, and maybe embed a YouTube Video	Page	113
Acknowledgements	Page	121

Don't just **Bitch**, **Moan**, **Whinge**.....
Keep Calm and Carry-on Complaining

Find out how you can take on the big guys and **WIN** when goods and services don't perform as expected

INTRODUCTION

We're living in the age of what marketers and brand owners call 'big data'. To you and me, as people who buy products and services from brands, this means the myriad of information they gather about our purchase behaviour, our online activity, our income level and other personal details, what papers we read, where we holiday, and if we have a cat or a canary. All this information enables brands to personalise their products and services and provide us consumers with – we're led to believe – an improved, personalised, experience. The hard reality is that they want loyalty from us because loyalty equals profit, and all this data gives them the opportunity to crunch our information into profiles of us to meet our needs (i.e. to create more items and experiences that tempt us to buy THEIR goods and services). Put bluntly, in today's digital age, if brands don't meet our expectations, they fail. Big data helps them meet those needs not just now, but in a world of increasing artificial intelligence based on big data, customer loyalty will become even more important for commercial success.

Brands use measures such as Customer Lifetime Value (CLV) and Customer Experience to calculate our value as customers to their brand, and measure their performance at meeting it. One often quoted statistic is that 72% of happy customers will share their experience with six other people (Esteban Kolsky). So, with all this clever thinking and marvellous data, you'd think then that there wouldn't be a need for this book, which looks at how I've taken on some of the world's largest brands for their faulty products, dire customer service and misleading advertising claims. If those companies valued my custom, and wanted me to be a loyal customer, or if they were able to easily measure my CLV (say for instance travel brand TUI where I've spent tens of thousands over the years), surely, they'd be responsive and keen to resolve my problems quickly so that I can carry on spending my hard earnt cash with them. In my experience, I'd say not a bit of it.

I'm not a brand guru, a solicitor, or a journalist. I'm a professional family man who over the years has bought cars, booked holidays and used computers, mobile phones and software. 99% of these activities have been and gone without the need to take pen to paper or fingers to keyboard to complain. But for the 1% that have, I'm glad to say I have a very good record of taking these large organisations to task and winning. What's the secret of my success? The power of YouTube and customised websites.

From www.mybmwexperience.co.uk to www.mysensatoriexperience.co.uk to www.wouldyoubuyatiguan.co.uk, publishing a YouTube video or customised website outlining the facts of my complaint has had a 100% success rate. So, I felt it was time I shared my learnings from taking on the big brands with you. It's surprisingly easy, extremely satisfying, and yes, it works.

When you read my experiences with brands including BMW and VW, TUI and Microsoft over the years, I am sure you'll recall similar times in your life when you've felt disappointed or even duped by a brand. This can make you angry, frustrated and in many cases, totally helpless. As one BMW customer expressed it, "I thought I was losing my marbles." If you've been bombarded with standard, *"There is nothing we can do"* responses to your letters, *"We have no control over this"* answers from call centres, or fobbed off by suited salesmen and officious customer service reps repeating the same mantra (aka 'like it or lump it'), I wouldn't blame you for giving up; thousands do.

But I say no to giving up.

If your complaint is truly justified, the key to success is getting your grievances known to those more senior than the so-called customer service teams along with a realisation that unlike almost any amount of negative reviews on internet sites such as Trustpilot, TripAdvisor, and J.D. Power, that a single-issue website offers a greater potential to adversely affect a company's reputation and therefore sales. I wish it were that simple as they'd just be guided to do the right thing to rectify the situation when things go wrong, but it seems that you are required to take a well-prepared fight to big corporations. Many consumers will calculate that some actions require a financial investment in solicitors and lawyers – with no guarantee of success – and therefore the price of trying might not justify even a successful outcome, especially if large amounts of time and effort are required.

In addition to their obligations under various acts of legislation, I believe that all the companies that I've campaigned against have a moral obligation to their customers to provide the goods and services as advertised. I am a realist. I know to err is human, but I'm not so keen on forgiving large corporations, especially if I've invested time and money in their product or service. For me, the measure of a company is not how well they perform when things go right – that's easy – it is how they behave when things go wrong and when the fault, the basis of my complaint, is of their own making.

If there's one message I want brands to take away from this book, it's this: if you've made a mistake, accept it, apologise immediately – and in a manner that conveys you really mean it - and put it right at once. Take ownership. Don't pull down the shutters, send templated responses refuting responsibility, and ignore it – and definitely don't lie (as you'll see happens amongst my examples). That just makes people upset – and worse, it makes them cross. I am sure the majority of customers who have a genuine complaint eventually give up in the face of what I call 'Company Protection Teams'. In this digital age, we as customers have much more power than we realise. Our business is valuable to the big brands, and we should all recognise that. Not to mention, we have access to social media where we can share our experiences – good and bad – plus consumer laws support us with the best legal and financial protection ever, and that means we can fight our own corner without incurring the costs of legal action.

As a customer with a genuine grievance, giving up or liking or lumping it should be firmly relegated to the past when brands made things for us to buy and we merely 'consumed' them when we saw their latest ad campaign. Today we are informed, discerning customers – with an enormous choice, and with a voice. This book is about providing you with the confidence to take on the big brands. Stand your ground. You can take control just as I have done, without being aggressive, or losing your rag, or resorting to legal action.

So, if you find yourself having a battle with BMW, a moan with Microsoft, a tussle with TUI or a vendetta against VW, read on. If you have a genuine complaint with the hard facts and evidence to support it – unembellished with innuendo, guess work and conspiracy theories – then you can make your own voice be heard by mega brands like these. I'm confident you can get the resolution you want with the power of YouTube videos and customised websites. As well as the examples in this book, which are all my own and I hope you will enjoy reading, Chapter Seven provides step-by-step advice for making a simple website and how to incorporate a YouTube video.

Lumped together in a single book, these complaints may at first sight seem to be those of a vexatious complainant. We all know that some people will complain not because they have received a particularly poor experience but because they know a claim is likely to succeed.

My experiences in this book span across 10 years. There have been many more times when myself or my family have received poor service, but on those occasions emails and letters did suffice and the situations were amicably rectified after people took ownership for them.

The examples in this book were not resolved with written words on a page but instead escalated to something more public. A little bit like the concept of the Academy Award winning film 'Three Billboards Outside Ebbing, Missouri,' where a mother rents three big billboards to name and shame the Police Chief for not adequately investigating the rape and murder of her daughter.

In the film, that public shaming spurs the police into action – for a far more serious reason than any of my complaints - which is exactly what my own methodology also achieves.

I've tried to bring a little bit of storytelling into situations that can be incredibly frustrating, and to bring some human interaction to the heart of these conversations that aim to explore and explain the context behind them.

COVID-19

The lockdown and confinement to home has given me both the opportunity and motivation to complete this book that has been two years in the planning and writing.

Sadly, the Chateau Impney (Experience Three) announced on Friday 3rd April 2020 that it has permanently closed. I have added an update to the end of that chapter.

There will be many business casualties as a result of this pandemic, and many of us will have long memories about the way companies dealt with their customers during this time.

I have three immediate examples to share, all relating to travel companies. In March, WizzAir cancelled our return flight from Krakow to Luton with barely 24 hours' notice. Their email notification on 14th March advised that details on a refund or voucher would be forthcoming within 14 days. Today is Friday 22nd May and so far nothing has been received from WizzAir. My only option is to call their contact centre - with reported stories of 80-minute wait times - at £1.49 per minute. No thank you.

On 2nd June I wrote to WizzAir's UK MD, who I tracked down on Companies House, and a week later I received a credit for future travel.

A family weekend in France scheduled for early April was cancelled because of lockdown. Having sent many emails to me offering to reschedule later in the year, on 20th March Ryanair formally cancelled the flights. Ryanair's email included a link to a refund or voucher for future travel, and the same day I opted for the refund and submitted my claim. I had an email on 28th March and again on the 9th of April informing me that my refund (£895.84) was being processed, but that COVID-19 was making this a longer process than usual.

On 20th April I received another email from Ryanair stating that my travel voucher, that I didn't request, will be valid until 18th April 2021.

For various reasons we can't reschedule our trip to Limoges and now having started a refund process over one month ago, to have this changed without any consultation into a voucher, will live long in my memory.

After Ryanair changed their initial promise of a refund to a voucher, I contacted my bank, Nationwide, to see if they could request a chargeback from Ryanair to my credit card. Finally, on 22nd June the refund from Ryanair arrived back in my account.

For the same weekend in Limoges, I had booked hotel rooms on a 'non-refundable' basis to get a better deal. Due to COVID-19, Accor hotels offered to move my booking to later in the year. When I explained to the hotel why it would not be possible, they refunded in full my non-refundable payment. I do use Accor hotels extensively; I have one of their loyalty cards, and I will be using it even more in the future.

Ryanair took my payment for flights immediately. It took them three months to provide a refund, during which time they changed their refund confirmation to a voucher adding that for anyone wanting a refund, "we will place your request in the cash refund queue until the COVID-19 emergency has passed." They only provided the refund because I requested the chargeback via my credit card.

This is an appalling way to treat customers, Especially one with a long history of booking hundreds of Ryanair flights!

Keep Calm – and Carry On Complaining!

Why Do I Complain?

Having written up all these experiences, I thought it might be useful, or at the very least interesting personally for me, to reflect on what drives me to take such companies and their initial reluctance to provide satisfactory customer service, to task.

I quickly concluded that my aims in all these situations was the often-used mantra, "Don't get mad, get even." In other words, I was just seeking compensation equal to the value of the perceived loss as a result of poor performance for goods and services that I had personally invested my money in.

I also want them to fully acknowledge their shortcomings with an apology.

I think there is more to it than just getting even. I've invested in the goods and services provided by these brands because they speak to my personality, my values, my aspirations. I want their products to be perfect; I want BMW cars to have faultless DAB radios and TUI's Sensatori brand to be even better than it is. In fact, with TUI, I've not only complained to them just so they can put it right, but I have also made suggestions for making Sensatori even better.

Apple, one of the biggest companies in the world, provides excellent customer service when things go wrong. You could argue that they charge a premium for their products and that part of this cost allows them to provide a great customer experience even when there is a technical failure. Shouldn't all companies operate in this way?

Investigative journalists tell of 'speaking truth to power' when they discover situations where they believe governments and individuals need their actions exposing to a wider audience. Whilst I don't for one moment suggest that my complaints exist in the same sphere as political and criminal offences, nevertheless I knew that the prospect of them becoming known to a wider audience would be negative publicity that surely any company would want to avoid?

When considering these aspects, it was then a challenge to determine whether this information would be more useful for the reader to know before they read the individual experiences, or as a summing up to the book as a whole. I determined that the former would provide more perspective and provide a back-story to each experience.

Rhetorically, I'd like to ask each reader, "What would you have done?"

There are two aspects to this.

1. Had you been in my shoes, would you have thought that each situation merited a proper complaint?
2. If you had been responsible for the customer service provision at each of these companies, what action would you have taken to provide me, assuming you deemed my complaint to be fully justified, with a suitable outcome?

A Genuine Complaint

This is the first thing that both the person sending a complaint and the receiver of the complaint need to determine. Is this a justifiable situation where the complaint being made requires a remedy?

That led me to ask myself, "What is a genuine complaint?"

I have come up with the following statement.

"Have I been provided with substandard goods or an inadequate service in a situation that could and should have been avoided?" In other words, am I assured that the provision of the goods and service to the level and quality reasonably expected, were fully within the control of the company supplying them, to have done so?

In all the cases raised in my book, I believe that the poor quality or service were fully within the powers of the company to avoid. There are circumstances when this is not possible, and so even though I have been inconvenienced, on such occasions I have not raised a complaint. There are three that come to mind, all coincidentally to do with travel. Twice in the last two years, adverse weather has resulted in severe delays to my return train travel from Scotland. The first, in June 2018, occurred when powerful storms resulted in power lines on the West Coast being damaged and I had to take three different trains across to and down the East Coast in order to get back to Birmingham – adding more than a couple of hours onto my journey. Also, the severe floods in December 2019 required diversions around affected areas, reduced speeds across the network, and caused numerous cancellations of services that resulted in standing room only from Glasgow to Droitwich. In neither of these cases did I determine a complaint to be in anyone's interest. The train companies did their best in circumstances outside their control, and although late, I did arrive home safely.

In March 2017, our Sunday evening return flight with EasyJet from Bilboa to London Luton was delayed beyond the two hours for compensation as a result of strike action by you know who, bloody French Traffic Controllers! Again. Other flights, such as a BA flight to Heathrow which had already boarded, were cancelled and so my companions and I were just incredibly pleased to not have the starts to our working week wrecked, although an extra night in Bilboa would have been great fun.

So now that I've determined that a complaint is necessary, how should businesses respond?

The Complaint Handling Strategy

Any company selling products or services to consumers is going to get complaints. Some forward-thinking companies recognise that unresolved complaints result in customers taking their business elsewhere. But, they will also know that if handled correctly, a complaint could be a great opportunity to achieve even greater loyalty from transforming negative situations into positive experiences for customers. It might also be an opportunity to genuinely improve whatever is being complained about to the benefit of the company.

Clearly you will not read about the companies that I've complained to and who have resolved my complaint on the receipt of the first email or letter. Sometimes, that complaint has resulted in the company explaining why my complaint is unfounded, and they have effectively educated me. I've appreciated their honesty whilst acknowledging my lack of knowledge. But mostly my complaints are fully justified, with resolutions offered and accepted.

I want the companies I complain to, to find a remedy because typically I want to carry on using their products. If I didn't care, or if the 'financial loss' was minimal, I almost certainly wouldn't bother with a complaint.

I am looking for them to:

- Respond quickly.
- Demonstrate that they have listened correctly and to either agree with my complaint, or to robustly defend it.
- Apologise as if they mean it, assuming my complaint is upheld by their internal scrutiny.
- Offer a quick resolution. I usually state in my complaint what a resolution looks like from my point of view with some explanation to justify for this. I have never asked for something that was impossible to deliver or which outweighed my loss.
- Learn from it. As I mentioned earlier, I want to carry on using these brands, so they need to ensure that product and service improvements can be put into place. They should also recognise that complaints can be an opportunity to learn about shortcomings with their products and services and that if

frequently occurring, improvements can be put into place to avoid future customer dissatisfaction.

I do not believe that I am someone who complains just for the sake of complaining; life is far too short for that. But when I take the time and trouble to complain properly, in a professional and polite way; and by this I mean an email or letter direct to the company and not just an angry unsubstantiated comment on social media, etc., then I expect a professional and robust response, not just a template document full of platitudes and fob-offs.

I am not attempting to get something for nothing, and for me a meaningful apology is a great place to start.

I have never threatened the use of a website to escalate my complaint. I want companies to rectify situations because of what has happened, not because of any threat of a more public exposure.

In most cases, I am not looking for this episode to be the last dealings that I have with this company.

Why Keep Me as A Customer?

Having investigated many different aspects of customer service for this book, there are some additional points, not specific to my experiences, that companies who provide poor customer service might like to consider.

It costs businesses considerably more in marketing spend to find new customers than retain existing ones. Companies such as KPMG, Gartner and the Harvard Business School all have reports highlighting the importance of retaining existing customers as a contribution to turnover and profit.

Internal morale can be negatively impacted by providing poor customer service too. Generally, people like to do a good job and treat customers fairly. If employees are being directed to provide a poor service and avoid resolutions at any cost, they will feel demoralised. The sales professional, who worked hard to get the company the business in the first place, will feel frustrated to lose the opportunity for returning customers if other parts of the business are jeopardising this future business for them. So, the cost of poor customer service is not just experienced by the customer, but it can have good people leave a company to work elsewhere too.

Experience One

My BMW Experience

(www.mybmwexperience.co.uk)

During the summer of 2014 I created an opportunity to leave full-time employment and set up my own business. By the end of the year I had secured some medium to long term contracts and after Christmas determined that I now needed to have a car of my own rather than pinch the wife's or hire one.   Many years earlier I'd briefly had a BMW as a company car, and the directors of my most recent employer raved about their BMWs whilst allocating a Ford Galaxy to me!

With a budget firmly in mind, my wife and I visited the local BMW dealer where many second-hand models gleamed brightly on their forecourt display in the cold February sunshine. When the inevitable silver-suited and Chelsea-booted salesman invaded our browsing, to answer his questions and confirmatory statements, I provided details on my maximum budget and unequivocally stated my three 'red-line' requirements. These were, in no particular order; leather seats, a DAB radio (because sadly I avidly listen to 5Live and regularly travel before dawn and after dusk when MW reception is appalling), and CO_2 emissions below a level that would make it tax advantageous for me whilst assisting the government to achieve its carbon reduction targets too.   There and then I test-drove an X1, their baby 4x4. Beautiful but, as it turned out, producing too many CO_2 emissions to satisfy both my accountant and the then Secretary of State for Energy and Climate Change.

Unbeknown to me, I now discovered that this dealer's network extended to another two garages some distance away and that any stock in those locations could magically appear for me to test drive locally.   By now it was closing time on the Sunday and the discussion continued over email for a few days, where thankfully I had reiterated my three 'red-line' requirements in writing.   The following weekend I went back to test drive a 1 series that met the three red-lines, was just within my budget, and with additional purchasing persuaders: low mileage, stunning Valencia orange paint, and an automatic sports gearbox. It didn't drive anywhere near as majestically as it looked, it was truly even better. My Ford was in a Galaxy far, far away.

My Orange Bullet! – Photo © Duncan Peberdy

I've already alerted you to the fact that I'm a bit of a nerd when it comes to listening to Radio 5 Live on Digital Radio. I even own a portable digital radio so that when I walk my dogs, I can keep up to date with what is going on in the world. This proved, as you will shortly read, to be a real advantage in the case of Peberdy v BMW when the latter decided not to treat me as a valued customer. Instead, they treated me as a mild-irritation or inconvenience, like something unpleasant on the bottom of your shoe that can happen when walking your dog and distracted by your crystal clear digital radio – as a result of another dog owner not being responsible and taking ownership for their dog, in the same way that no one at BMW ever took credible ownership of my situation and addressed my complaint.

So, what was that situation and how did BMW react?

With frustrating regularity, the DAB radio in my orange bullet kept cutting out and instead of the 'enhanced audio clarity' alluded to in BMW's advertising, I got a few seconds of silence accompanied by the now tragically familiar 'No Signal' appearing on the radio display.

Somewhat ironically, at the same time I was experiencing the poor DAB performance in my 1 Series, BMW were actively promoting in a dedicated brochure on in-car entertainment that BMW DAB Digital Radios provide:

1.'A wider variety of radio stations with enhanced audio quality.'

2.'Enhanced audio clarity' (just in case it wasn't clear in point 1).

So, here's the thing. I may have been new to owning (on finance) a BMW, but I wasn't at all new to having my cars equipped with a DAB radio. Previous company cars, including a VW Passat, AUDI A4 and even my 'care-in-the-community bus' disguised as a Ford Galaxy, each had a DAB radio. They all lost signal in the far-flung corners of North Wales, the Lake District, the Scottish Boarders and Highlands (I told you I did a lot of business travelling), but they never lost signal in my home town, on the M40 through Oxfordshire or on the M6 heading north to Manchester or Liverpool. Yet on these regular journeys in my little orange bullet, whilst still travelling within national speed limits for those roads, the DAB radio would cut out. Just at a time when the football scores were being announced; Nottingham Forest 2, Blackpool .... and then silence and the outcome unknown. Or, at a time when the cricket test match score was being updated. It's funny how it genuinely always seemed to be at a time when some important piece of information was being deliberately withheld from me. Perhaps I'm being unfair to BMW, perhaps it was really highly advanced artificial intelligence at work and saving me from learning that my football team had just been beaten so as to keep me in a good mood for a little while longer. But I don't think so.

Frustrated, frustrated, frustrated. In fact, so frustrated that keeping count of how many times the BMW DAB radio cut out on a single journey, became a bit of a game to pass the time. On one occasion in 2015 I drove from my home in Droitwich, down the M40, round the M25 to Cobham, then across to Basingstoke, and back to Droitwich. I logged all the points of the nine occasions on this 265-mile journey when my BMW DAB radio lost reception. The following Wednesday, I again travelled down the M40, this time to Bagshot before returning home - total 250 miles. On this day the DAB reception was lost on seven occasions – all at different points along the M40 to the journey the previous week. These were identical journeys to business contacts that I have made in my Ford Galaxy, my Audi A4, and my VW Passat, and not once had the DAB radios cut-out during previous identical drives in those non-BMW cars.

I went back to my authorised BMW dealer, told them about the DAB experiences in my 1 Series, and was met with statements about the poor quality of DAB transmission in the UK being to blame. "Ah, not so quick," I said. Surely, if the DAB transmission is the problem here, then why have I not had any problems with the DAB quality in my previous cars, at which point I explained what you have just read.

"Mmmmm" they muttered. Followed by "Well it could be a problem with the aerial in your car," they finally espoused after trying to think a little about the interesting conundrum I had just explained to them. They determined to take my car off the road for a day – with the inconvenience of not supplying a courtesy replacement for my troubles of their making – so they could replace the rear window that I now discovered contained the digital aerial.

On the back of accusations about poor quality DAB transmission, Mr Google and I researched the DAB transmitters on the UK Digital Radio website and discovered that they do indeed vary, but around Worcestershire and the West Midlands we are served by some of the most powerful there are in the UK.

Did the new rear window with its in-built aerial make a difference? Of course not. But if I now had a super-duper new aerial (the original one was only 15 months old) and the DAB transmission quality had not affected my other cars, the problem still had to be with the DAB receiver in my BMW. Obviously. My local dealer spoke to BMW, BMW UK allegedly spoke to BMW technicians in Germany, and the upshot was to inconvenience me for a further two days whilst they took DAB reception data from my DAB unit and analysed it. Seriously? Why not just change the DAB unit in my car to solve the problem? I offered it as a remedy. They had my car for two days, without supplying a courtesy replacement for my troubles which were of their making, and the data was analysed.

After two days of collecting and analysing clinical DAB data, my BMW was declared fit and healthy. There was, I was told both verbally and in writing, nothing wrong with the DAB unit in my car. It met all of BMW's manufacturing standards and therefore there was absolutely nothing that BMW could now do. Have your car back and like it or lump it. Well I certainly didn't like it, and I definitely wasn't going to put up with it.

Let's Make a YouTube Video

Having a DAB radio was one of only three must-haves 'red-line' requirements that I'd troubled my local BMW authorised dealer to concern themselves with. I wrote to BMW Customer Service, I wrote to BMW Finance and I wrote to BMW Quality Standards to reject the car because it did not, in my opinion, meet expectations. Under consumer law, goods and services must fit the description, and the provision of DAB was set out clearly, in writing, prior to purchase, as one of just three 'red-line' requirements I had for my new car.

Somewhat astoundingly, BMW Quality Service replied in writing to say (and acknowledge) that although I had requested a DAB radio at the time of purchase, I hadn't specified what the quality of it should be. This is from the company that claims to provide the 'Ultimate Driving Machine' with no caveat that I am aware of about it not applying to some models, features or specifications, and with a worldwide reputation for excellence. Don't forget that at this time BMW was proactively promoting the 'enhanced audio quality' from having a DAB radio in their cars. You would have thought, or at least I thought, that BMW would want to live up to their crystal clear and unambiguous marketing claims.

Prior to what was about to happen, BMW made no offer to truly rectify the situation, to admit that my car's DAB was performing poorly, or to compensate me in some way. They continued to blame the UK's DAB transmission and I think both BMW and their authorised reseller just hoped that I would put up, shut up, and leave them alone if they could fob me off for long enough. They were about to learn that I don't do 'fobbed-off.'

I wasn't getting driving pleasure – or 'Freude am Fahren' as they advertise the attributes of BMW on their German-speaking websites, nor was I getting any sense of concern or customer service locally or from BMW UK's Customer Service team, which I subsequently renamed as BMW's Company Protection Team. Still to this day, some five years later, I cannot believe that BMW:

- Haven't thanked me for bringing the sub-standard quality of their UK DAB equipment to their attention and proved this in such a way that they can improve future production.
- Never once apologised as if they meant it.
- Didn't offer some recompense that would have stopped the situation, cost them less money, and avoided all the negative publicity. They could have installed an after-market DAB, perhaps one manufactured by Pure, or given me a connector for my iPhone (no Apple Car Play on a 2014 model), or maybe offered me something like a BMW bike or bike rack. They never once asked me for a suggestion as to what happiness might look like for me as a resolution to the issue.
- No longer wanted me as a BMW customer.

What, BMW no longer wanted you (and your money) as a customer.

They said that. Really?

Remember, my approved used BMW was not purchased from a back-street garage, an auction, or a private seller that might conveniently overlook some minor defect that is not visually obvious, but from an authorised dealer with multiple garages equipped to BMW's exacting standards and a full member of BMW's Approved Used BMW sales. The benefit, as it states on their website, of buying an 'approved used BMW is that "You can be assured of sheer driving pleasure and complete peace of mind with our comprehensive range of additional benefits." When claiming that they are providing 'The Ultimate Driving Machine' (on BMW's UK website) or merely 'Freude am Fahren' on their German site, which translates as "Driving Pleasure," BMW should protect their brand simply by living up to the expectations for quality and driving pleasure that they themselves have set unequivocal expectations for.

Finally, that YouTube Video

Earlier I told you that I was a bit of a nerd when it comes to DAB digital radio, and that I have a portable one that I used to educate myself with world affairs when I'm out walking my dogs. What if that £70 battery-operated radio would work in my BMW when their crystal-clear DAB failed? Now that would prove one thing beyond any doubt, that the problem wasn't one of UK DAB transmission, and that the 'No Signal' message on the radio screen was in fact 'no reception' which may result in the same outcome, but which in fact is a totally different circumstance causing the problem I had now experienced over and over and over and over again. Except on the M40 when it was, over, and over and over and over and over and over and over and over and over and over and over again.

I connected my £70 Pure Move 2500 portable digital radio up to an external speaker, tuned this and my BMW radio to Steve Wright in the Afternoon, and set off on a local journey from home, in a built-up area of the West Midlands where NONE of my previous DAB-equipped cars had failed my DAB listening pleasure. My daughter sat in the passenger seat and used my iPhone to record the status of what happened. Coincidentally, 'Digging Your Scene' with Dr. Robert on lead vocals, is one of my favourite Blow Monkey's tunes from the 80s, and as we started our journey it was playing on Radio 2.

I think you're ahead of me now; a bit like when someone puts all their words on a PowerPoint slide, and you've scanned to the end before they have read verbatim to even half-way! You are not wrong. You will need to watch and more importantly listen for just 2 minutes and 25 seconds before the BMW radio loses reception and the inexpensive Pure portable radio continues to give me one of my favourite songs. National DAB radio in a built-up area without the presence of hills or valleys fails to be received by the 'meets all manufacturing standards' of the ultimate driving machine and yet continues efficiently on an inexpensive portable radio powered by a small rechargeable battery. This wasn't a second, third or fourth making of the video. This was two minutes and 25 seconds after the very first journey started with the portable radio and the iPhone.

As a little aside, shortly before Christmas 2018 my DAB Move 2500 gave up the ghost after many years of almost daily service and guess what I've replaced it with? Right again, a Pure DAB Move R3 that for under £90, provides an even more crystal-clear listening experience than the previous one.

What Did BMW Experience of Me?

I have to think that BMW thought my initial complaint was just a case of BMW v BMW. i.e. my Bitching, Moaning, Whinging v a major global corporation with both a customer protection squad and an irrefutable

Quality Standards Team. I'm sure that they thought I would soon "go away."

Long before I got to the stage of capturing compelling video evidence, I had telephoned and emailed the local BMW dealer who had sold me my BMW in order to find a resolution. A contractual factor is that I used BMW Finance to 'buy' my orange bullet, and so I emailed and wrote to BMW Finance, along with BMW Quality Standards, BMW's Managing Director, and BMW Customer Service who, in my opinion, had all been culpable at different stages for not sorting this out. None of these people wanted to accept that there was a problem and then to try to find a way to resolve the situation. Time and time again I asked BMW to replace the DAB unit in my car, but I can now deduce that BMW knew full well that there was a problem with the DAB reception in some of their vehicles and that a replacement like-for-like unit wasn't going to solve the problem. Many people who contacted me as a result of my next action, wrote to me with similar examples from their own BMW experience, which clearly (but not crystal clearly) wasn't limited to only the 1 Series models. What did I do? Bear with.

With my little iPhone video up on YouTube I sent the good people at BMW in the UK und auch in Deutschland a link to it. Without any other promotion or keywords or metatags (the techy things that would help anyone searching for BMW or DAB radio to find it) it quickly got a few dozen views; people who had received that link were watching it. If you search hard enough, you can find the email address for senior people working for almost any company. Today, many companies protect this information rigorously, but in 2015 it was less difficult to find. Many companies have separate websites containing their corporate and investor information, with product information, retail locations, etc., on their more public site. For example, www.bmw.de is BMW's site for cars, whilst www.bmwgroup.com is where you will find information on Investor Relations, Corporate Responsibility, Innovation, etc.

I sent my email containing a link to the YouTube video to dozens of people in senior positions at BMW in the UK, in France, Switzerland, the USA, etc., and at their headquarters in Germany. But although I could see the video was getting views, there was still no direct response from anyone at BMW to it. Being impulsive and with a low boredom threshold, after a few days, I created a website to highlight my poor experience with BMW and embedded my illuminating video into it.

www.mybmwexperience.co.uk

The factual story of unacceptable DAB radio quality in my 1 Series BMW was now hosted for the world to read, along with MY little video to prove the point that was, for far too long, being ignored by BMW. Not anymore.

My story is not embellished at any stage with innuendo, guess work or conspiracy theories; it only states the truth, all of which can be evidenced fully in letters, emails, and recordings of meetings with the Sales Manager and Service Manager at my local fully-authorised BMW dealer; both of whom were incidentally nice people and even fully acknowledged that my DAB problem was not at all news for themselves or BMW. Who would have known differently about DAB transmission being the supposed culprit if you hadn't experienced a perfectly good DAB system before?

As a result of my website, other BMW owners, many of whom had DAB systems in their previous cars, some of which were BMW cars and some of which were other brands, now contacted me as they had encountered the same problem and had been thus far fobbed-off by BMW in the same manner that BMW had initially tried with me. Some were die-hard BMW drivers who had driven nothing else for many years and who were now treated with the same shocking disinterest by BMW.

Would Your Mother be Ashamed of You?

The very same people at BMW whose latest letter a few days previously had stated the following, now asked my local authorised reseller to negotiate a settlement with me on their behalf.

"As I've advised previously, Rybrook Worcester [my local authorised reseller] have confirmed that your car radio is working to BMW standards. We wouldn't be able to replace your radio with an upgraded audio system or offer any compensation, because we're happy that the radio in your car is acting as it should be.

I believe we've made our position clear and we're unable to change this. I'm sorry that any further responses won't bring this matter to a close in the way that you'd hoped."

What were they prepared to do? This was not about money. They could have sorted this out at the outset if they had apologised, admitted that there was a problem that couldn't be directly sorted, and had offered me something to compensate. iPhone connectivity, a BMW cycle or cycle carrier perhaps; we will never know because they never took any genuine interest to solve my poor experience in this way.

So, it wasn't about money, it was about lying to me, about not taking ownership of the problem, and not wanting to do anything until I had escalated my complaint to a website containing compelling video evidence. And most of all it was about the lack of a proper apology at any stage. Even now!

I asked them to take back the car and refund me everything I had paid; the deposit plus ten months of finance payments. They initially offered less than half this amount, but crucially didn't ask me at any stage during the negotiations to take down the website. They clearly didn't want to make the refund and take back the car as I was asking, but I stood my ground and reluctantly to BMW they eventually met my requirement of them.

Earlier I alluded to the fact that, in my opinion, the BMW Customer Service Team should be re-branded as the BMW Company Protection Team. In all their dealings with me, they never once gave me the impression that they were bothered about me, their customer. Other people who contacted me with the same problem and getting the same short-shrift from the Company Protection Team at BMW prompted me to ask BMW staff if "Their mother would be ashamed of them" for the way that they were (being instructed, no doubt,) dealing with the very genuine problems that their customers were having with their DAB radios? I also wonder what job satisfaction such people have when they are seemingly restricted from correcting poor customer experiences?

BMW Don't Want me as a Customer!

Yes really. Now we had got to the stage of BMW agreeing a full refund, I asked if instead I could put this money towards a deal for a BMW X1 – their baby 4 x 4. There was now a model that had the CO_2 emissions below 'accountant-level' that I had my eye on. This was on the basis that the DAB-experience aside, the BMW was everything I thought that it would be and my business was doing well. I clearly knew up front and accepted that there could be a DAB issue, but almost 12 months on, in-car connectivity to iPhones had advanced massively and DAB was not so important to me. What happened next frankly astounded me.

Rob, the Sales Manager and a really nice guy at my local BMW reseller, told me that this would not be possible as he had been instructed by BMW UK (don't forget he was the negotiating face of BMW UK and BMW Finance) that they no longer wanted me as a BMW customer. Gulp. All I had tried to do was get a working DAB with uninterrupted crystal-clear audio in my BMW car, and perhaps even help BMW improve their manufacturing quality for future drivers. That's really quite admirable, no?

An End Point Reached

BMW had their 1 Series car back.

BMW Finance fully refunded my initial deposit and every monthly finance payment made, and the finance agreement effectively 'written off.'

My website that alerts people to my experience with BMW continues to be hosted. BMW never stipulated its removal as part of the 'deal' reached, and it's my little homage to not being wanted as a BMW customer and for BMW having never properly said "sorry."

Oh, and as an example of my digital skills and an opportunity to use the German that I learnt when I was somewhat ironically a resident for two years in Munich, the home of BMW, there is now a German version of my website www.meinebmwerfahrung.com.

Together, these two websites cost me about £7 per month to keep alive. Less than the cost of a couple of pints in London or Munich, and much better for my well-being. I am now hopeful that this will not have been a cost but will instead prove to be an investment for me given the contribution that 'myBMWexperience' has added to this book.   In addition, every Monday morning I get two emails from my web hosting company with the previous week's visitor statistics from the German and English versions of my website. They inform me about the number of unique visitors to my websites, where in the world the people looking are located at the time they accessed the website, and which search engine assisted them. In a typical week, the English version gets 54 hits and the German version 45. During 2019, in addition to the UK and Germany, my websites have been accessed by people in the following places. USA, China, Belgium, Netherlands, France, Russia, Canada, Denmark, Norway, Brazil, Spain, and Portugal.

My little video clearly highlighting the quality of an inexpensive portable PURE DAB radio has now had over 8,100 views.

I've also taken the opportunity to write directly with my experience of poor customer service to people who should care about BMW; so far, I haven't received any responses from them. People such as Suzanne Klatten and Stefan Quandt, both long term investors and board members at BMW, and a small selection of sports professionals and celebrities in the UK and Germany who act, or have previously acted, as brand ambassadors for BMW.

All for a DAB Radio?

Well you could look at it like that, but for BMW the digital components of their vehicles continue to be of high importance.

BMWs are about driving pleasure and when we are travelling in a BMW should we not be able to enjoy the digital lifestyle that we take for granted elsewhere in our lives?

BMW absolutely agree; the following quote is taken from their website. "Why compromise when traveling? Enjoy the digital lifestyle you are used to in your BMW as well."

(Source: https://www.bmw.de/de/topics/faszination-bmw/connecteddrive/bmw-connected-drive-uebersicht.html#connected_drive_packages accessed on 18th January 2019 with Google auto translate.)

In their letter dated 3rd September 2015 when BMW Quality Standards again put in writing that as far as they were concerned there was nothing wrong with the DAB in my car and that they were "unable to agree to the rejection of your vehicle on this basis," They then added that "under the terms of our Complaints Procedure, this is our final response." Adding that if I was unhappy with it, I could refer my complaint to the Financial Ombudsman Service, which was free of charge and had to be submitted with six months. On 10th September 2015 I submitted a complaint form to the Financial Ombudsman Service, which again gave my preferred remedy to have a BMW with a fully working DAB radio or, failing that, to receive a full refund. To date, I have not had any response from the Financial Ombudsman Service.

Other Drivers with Unacceptable DAB Equipment in their BMWs

www.mybmwexperience.co.uk not only contained the story of my own experience with BMW, but also asked for anyone else with a similar experience to get in touch. From those that responded, the story was essentially the same; unacceptably poor digital radio performance being blamed on UK DAB transmission, even to people, who like me had previously owned other vehicles with DAB radios that had performed perfectly in the same places that their BMW DAB was now losing signal.

BMW 3 Series M Sport

When this driver – who incidentally bought his vehicle from a different garage owned by the same dealer that I purchased mine from – was getting nowhere after the dealer had retained his car on several occasions to try and establish the cause, he decided to drive it to BMW's UK Head Office in Farnborough without appointment and was finally able to speak to BMW's national service manager about it after the UK managing director would not come and speak to him. After a further four weeks of the car being at the local dealer, they declared that nothing could be done, and he was then offered a refund and an additional £2,000 towards another BMW and opted for a BMW 5 Series. That has also been a "terrible experience" for other reasons, and in January 2019 when I caught up with him, he concluded with "I wouldn't ever buy another BMW again. They would have sent me packing if I hadn't have gone to Farnborough. I even said to Paul xxxx [the national service manager] that I was ready to drive the car to Munich and park it in the most awkward place and walk away from it because that's how much I hated BMW at the time, and I would have as well."

BMW X5

In 2017, this driver commented to me:

"First off thank you for creating your web-page I'm a lot happier now that I'm not losing my marbles! My 2010 X5 radio works fine in MW and FM but is a complete nightmare in DAB. Not for me it drifting in and out of signal ... Every time the car is stopped for more than 30 minutes it loses signal where before it worked and won't come back on again for 45 mins. After 35-45 mins if I jiggle round the stations searching for a signal it suddenly bursts into life and then almost as suddenly ALL the stations work."

BMW advised that this was an issue caused by a low-battery, but replacing the battery didn't solve it, and BMW just kept wanting HIM to throw money at it.

Between him and his wife, over the last 22 years they have owned 14 BMWs, but when I caught up with him in January 2019, he told me that "I now have a Porsche Cayenne which, while not as fast as the X5, gives me a lot more peace of mind."

BMW X3 M Sport

In August 2017, the driver of this vehicle also had some issues with unacceptable miles per gallon as well as the same DAB experience of my own car. The dealer had this new car for 5 days before offering the same explanations about the DAB. The complaint escalated to the customer service team at BMW'S UK HQ, who still initially offered no remedy and pointed the owner in the direction of the Motor Ombudsman.

Eventually, "after quite a fight" to get a refund, and after referencing my website, this owner felt that he had "given in" when BMW offered him free access to their on-line music package which he adds that he has "thoroughly enjoyed."

However, when I caught up with him in January 2019, he added, "I will seriously rethink purchasing BMW again though after the way I was treated - for that there is no excuse!"

I add no personal comment or opinion to these examples from some of the many people who contacted me after seeing my website.

Key **B**its of **M**agic and **W**isdom from my BMW experience

- Always put your baseline requirements in writing – you may need this later.
- When writing to complain, refer to the brand's advertising claims.
- Research the key executives online, send letters and emails and get read receipts on the latter.
- Keep a diary of your issues and how they were dealt with.
- Invite other people to share their experiences – I have learnt in all my examples the complaints were never unique to me.
- Keep calm and complain effectively.

Experience Two

TUI's Broken Sensatori Promise

(www.mysensatoriexperience.co.uk)

Transforming a standard negative 'there is nothing we can do' response into £1500 compensation

Summary

TUI – The Company that, according to its massive investment in aspirational TV advertising, provides a great personalised holiday experience because they "Cross the 'T'S, dot the 'I's, and put 'U' in the middle." Which is great if you don't mind your acronyms being jumbled up!

With such a clearly stated and widely-broadcast whole-company focus for creating great personalised customer experiences, what could possibly go wrong on our much-anticipated holiday?

In 2018 my wife and I had a summer holiday to TUI's Sensatori resort in Mexico. Unfortunately, our holiday experience just wasn't as advertised in their brochure or on their website and so after we returned, I formally complained in writing to TUI. I was seeking some verification that TUI had been both morally and legally misleading and asking for them to rectify our poor experience and financially compensate us for **their** shortcomings, but TUI were having none of it. After receiving several, what seemed like, cut and pasted impersonal template replies containing only standard fob-off statements, the time had come to create a single-issue website to promote our poor holiday experience to senior management within TUI equipped with the authority to take full ownership and with the ability to rectify the situation.

The result: TUI's "After Travel Customer Support" team had originally replied several times with the standard "there is nothing more we can do" and "we have no control over this" and "we will definitely share your comments with the relevant team," but once my website was published and the details of my grievances were available for a much wider audience to read, TUI very quickly offered £1,500.00 compensation in the form of a voucher for a future holiday. There was also the option to choose a reduced value settlement in cash but, unlike BMW, the offer of a voucher did at least confirm that TUI still wanted our future custom.

Here's the full story.
The third Monday each January is designated, according to research undertaken by psychologist Dr Cliff Arnall back in 2005, as statistically the most depressing day of the year. Christmas and New Year have gone by in a flash, most of us have overspent, maybe we are in jobs when we would prefer a different one, and we leave home for and return from work in a world framed by a shortage of sunlight hours. We desperately need a holiday. Or at least we need to book a holiday and have something wonderful to look forward to. And it was literally three days after what has now become known as 'Blue Monday' and another of those sunlight-deficient days in January 2018, when my wife and I decided to book our next TUI Sensatori holiday adventure. Long haul to Mexico. Olé.

If Marks and Spencer did an advert for holidays, it wouldn't of course be an ordinary holiday it would be one in a five star resort, with a quality of entertainment befitting the West-End, with Heston Blumenthal food (there really was a Heston Blumenthal themed restaurant at the Sensatori in Mexico, although I recognise fully that Heston Blumenthal would be more akin to Waitrose than M&S), with the peace and quiet only spoilt by the distractions of a Downward Facing Dog and the controlled breathing accompanying it on the relaxation platform – assuming you were up early enough and on the beach. The beach, quite naturally, would be white sands lapped by warm turquoise water, because that was the two-page image portrayed in the Sensatori brochure we chose our holiday from. In the theatre of my own mind, that M&S advert would pretty much summarise our many positive personal experiences of Sensatori resorts – before the summer of 2018 that is.

Photo of the TUI brochure © Duncan Peberdy

WOW! Look at the white sand and turquoise sea just footsteps from the resort!

Sensatori is one of TUI's premium brands where for us personally, the expectations for relaxation and refuelling your senses, balanced leisure activities, (including the daily Yoga and Pilates on the relaxation platform I alluded to), the sophisticated dining and high-quality West End-esque entertainment, are well known. TUI themselves use the tagline,

"*Sensatori – luxury holidays designed to fuel the senses*," and, if we've had a good year financially, then the indulgence of a swim-up room directly from our room's patio, with all-inclusive drinks service, never fails to please. Yes, we are Sensatori junkies; it just works for us; a great mix of ignoring the rest of the world and joining in with only what we want to do. No entertainment team running around the pool with a whistle drumming up victims for pool polo, volleyball, or the like. It is all there to do if you want, but it's your choice and you can find it all on the iPhone App without any whistles or shouting or even without leaving your sunbed.

We are not the only couple who now plan our summer holiday around a Sensatori resort in order to soak up sunshine and refuel our senses! We've been to Sensatori resorts in Cyprus, Ibiza, Egypt, and Crete (twice), often bumping into people we recognised from other Sensatori resorts. When chatting to all these experienced Sensatori travellers, for those who had been there, Mexico always came out recommended as the 'best one yet.' We – and especially my wife – had Mexico on our Sensatori-to-do list, but only if we could get away for two weeks, which sadly isn't always the case. But how could it possibly be better than the Sunset bar in Cyprus, the Comedy Club in Crete, the highly-attentive pool-side drinks service in Egypt, or the outside adults-bar in Ibiza with its resident DJ getting us chilled as the sun and its residual heat fades beyond the waterline, that could possibly justify the inconvenience of a long-haul flight? "The food, the people, the weather," we kept getting told, especially when it's out of season for Europe. We were going in July.

Know your rights: The consumer protection bit

Before you learn what actually did go wrong, here's the consumer protection science (law) bit behind it all.

Whilst 1992 seems almost prehistoric for regulating an industry so disrupted by technology, technology that virtually everyone has in their pocket, whether using a mobile device or a PC, will increasingly use to book their holiday as more and more companies push us to their websites, there was no excuse in 2018 for companies such as TUI not to provide a customer experience that adheres to the minimum legal rights set out in the following Act of Parliament.

Package Travel, Package Holidays and Package Tours Regulations 1992

This law should ensure that the organiser, in this case TUI as the tour operator, does not provide misleading information and where there are any changes to that advertised, they must be provided to the customer as soon as possible. When these elements are not followed, the customer (me and my wife) are entitled to redress as follows:

> Loss of Value: being the difference between the cost you paid for the holiday and what you actually received. [And as you will read shortly, this can be a really subjective view and open to many differences in opinions.]
>
> Out-of-Pocket expenses for reasonable costs as a result of the breach of contract. [This I didn't know until researching this book; it might have been interesting if I had done so at the time.]
>
> Loss of Enjoyment; compensation for the disappointment and distress caused by things going wrong.

Under this law, the tour operator (TUI) is also legally responsible when the hotel or other services that they have contracted to fulfil its stated services to their customers do not perform as advertised.

As we boarded the TUI Dreamliner at Manchester airport for our two-week Sensatori holiday in Mexico, being experienced and loyal Sensatori regulars my wife and I thought we knew exactly what we were in for. The main attraction being the famous Riviera Maya with it's 'white sands and warm seas' lapping our resort. Our snorkels, flippers and face masks were packed.

The Riviera Maya near Cancun is well known by people who, like me, read the travel sections in Sunday papers but have never yet been, for being Caribbean-esque with mile after mile of white sandy beaches lapped by crystal clear waters. Although it was many years ago and when we had the kids in tow, we'd been to Jamaica and experienced sitting for hours in shallow sandy waters with a book and a drink. Even after our experience and compensation months earlier, and the poor experiences of many others posted on TripAdvisor as you will read, one of the headline facts that was still appearing on the TUI website for their Sensatori in Mexico when this chapter was first drafted on 09.03.2019, stated:

> *"One of the main draws of TUI Sensatori Resort Riviera Cancun is its setting. The resort is on the Riviera Maya, which means you're only ever footsteps from white sands and warm waters."*

[Note; when the TUI website was accessed on 15th October 2019, the words 'white sands' had (finally) been removed from the above sentence.]

Let's be clear [unlike the water], at the time we booked our Mexican holiday, before we left for Mexico and for almost 12 months after we returned, the promotional headlines TUI were using clearly stated: "White sands and warm water."

Our Mexican reality: Tons and tons of rotten stinking seaweed constantly blighting the shoreline and turning the sea brown, all of which requires a small private army of wheelbarrows and tractors trundling back and forth along the shoreline, all day – every day, just to keep the incessant seaweed from becoming a mountain.

To clarify, my issue is not with the seaweed itself; it is after all a naturally growing part of the ocean's ecology, and I have subsequently read that the volumes of seaweed can fluctuate from day to day. Indeed, we witnessed this ourselves where on one day the blanket of seaweed can stretch almost 100m, and the next only 10m. But the real problem is that the sea becomes brown as the seaweed decomposes rapidly in the tropical heat. Hence the colour of the water and hence the stench produced. That stench, by the way, doesn't stay on the beach, it permeates through the resort. When you exit the air-conditioned bubble of your hotel room first thing in the morning in search of breakfast, it hits you, especially, if like us, your room is the fourth one closest to the beachfront.

There was no point complaining at the time; there was nothing that could be done beyond what the hotel was already doing, and this problem affects every beachfront hotel along the same coastline for hundreds of miles and into many other countries too. At our resort, around 15 men were employed full-time to remove the seaweed, each with one wheelbarrow that once full had to be taken several hundred metres back along the beach so it could be taken off the beach at the point where the hotel complex ended. They did this from before 9am until late afternoon, every day. Aiding them, but not helping us, was a tractor that could enter the gently lapping shallow water with a trailer that mechanically raked up much more than all the wheelbarrows put together. It didn't help us because you had a diesel vehicle chugging along the seafront all day, and as it raked up the seaweed, it exacerbated the stench as the rotting seaweed was lifted.

An Army of Wheelbarrows! – Photo © Duncan Peberdy

So, you can see the beachfront disruption, but you can't smell it. Just how do you convey the Sensatori seaweed stench in a letter?

My letters and emails to TUI were effectively being ignored; yes, I eventually got replies, but only the usual fob-off platitudes about bringing my concerns to the attention of the right people (no names, no pack drill!) and no smell of any compensation to rectify a situation that TUI could have avoided.

The next step: build a website

TUI had been given several opportunities to take ownership and make the poor experience smell a little better. THEY had chosen not to do so, and so it was time for me to transition from the exchange of letters and emails to create a website where all the facts and only the facts, could reach a bigger audience and hopefully someone with some responsibility for the reputation of TUI, and more importantly to me, their customer, someone who would initiate the redress I wanted.

The website – www.mysensatoriexperience.co.uk - somewhat crudely made the following, unpolished suggestion, in order for on-line visitors to better understand the stench that on occasions induced the gagging reflex. Whereas my letter only incorporated some photos, the website that hosted my complaint about our experience in Mexico also contained a short video of the tractor churning up the seaweed. Perhaps not my finest hour, but in a highly digital world not yet able to convey the sense of smell over distance, I had a go at getting the real-life experience across.

> "*Before you see this short video of the tractor dredging the white sands and warm waters, you need to go to your downstairs loo, do a No. 2 and leave it for a couple of hours without flushing the loo or spraying air freshener! Now take your iPad into the loo to watch this video and you will get a sense of the smell that permeates the air as the tractor churns the seaweed."*

Walking north up the coastline, past three or four hotels all similarly blighted with seaweed, about a mile from our hotel were two turtle nests protected with cages and with signs informing about their expected hatching – which was anytime NOW. Each afternoon we strolled up the beach, camera in hand, hoping to experience infant turtles breaking free from their sandy womb. Sadly, we didn't get to witness this, nor to see the turtles quickly disappearing into brown water submerged beneath a carpet of floating seaweed, but it did mean that everyday I had my camera with me. I never had the thought of purposely 'collecting evidence' whilst we were there, but I am so glad that those baby turtles meant I had the camera, and that the wheelbarrows and tractors were amongst the many things that I thought it would be interesting to capture. I have a great photo from a Welsh university café where the warning sign by the milk flasks thankfully advises coffee lovers that the milk contains milk, just in case anyone with an allergy to something in milk, or with maybe just an irrational aversion to the colour of milk, isn't in any doubt. Oh, and at Wembley as you get your half-time cup of Bovril, tea or coffee, which are incidentally the only drinks available from this small vendor of hot drinks, the large helpful A4 printed sign advises, "Take Care! – All hot drinks contain hot liquid." Well who knew! And, it was a Spurs home game!

Back to my seaweed experience in Mexico and the un-augmented reality of the local situation.

White Sand and Turquoise Sea? – Photo © Duncan Peberdy

In researching my argument with TUI in connection with the seaweed in Mexico, I have accessed and read some websites where companies attempt to protect their individual positions and reputations by advising that this natural occurrence, most likely a direct consequence of rising ocean temperatures caused by global warming, as a 'force majeure.' Or in other words, as a 'chance occurrence' or 'unavoidable accident,' it's beyond our control, (which I wholeheartedly agree it is), as the law states that a Force Majeure is when unforeseeable circumstances prevent someone from fulfilling a contract. Of course, who doesn't have a Force Majeure clause in their contracts? TUI does, it's on page 84 of the July 2017 brochure for Sensatori holidays between November 2017 and October 2018. That's the very brochure we booked our holiday from and it reads:

Important Note – Events Beyond Our Control

Events beyond our control include war, threat of war, riots…….. natural and nuclear disasters, …. and any other similar events.

Amongst the same pages, headed "**Our Agreement with you, and yours with us**," in Clause 6, TUI state:

"If any part of your holiday is not provided as described and this spoils your holiday, we will pay you compensation, if appropriate, unless this is due to reasons beyond our control. See Important Notice – Events Beyond Our Control."

Four pages earlier in the small print section amongst the A-Z guide, under the heading Accuracy, the following statement is made:

"We published this brochure in July 2017. We always check our properties regularly to make sure we're giving you accurate information and we'll tell you about any major changes we're aware of as soon as we can."

Now this usually applies to situations such as major construction of a new neighbouring hotel, and further down the TUI A-Z Guide under the section "Building Work," TUI's position is:

> *"From time to time, building work is unavoidable, particularly where hotels are open all year round, and it can be noisy. If we're aware of any work, we'll let you know as soon as possible if we think it will affect your holiday. This can be difficult as we don't control the work and we're not always told when it will happen and how long it will last. But if we think it will have significant effect, you'll have the option of a refund or an alternative holiday, as outlined under 'Major Change to your Holiday' in Our Agreement With You."*

My wife and I were not aware of the seaweed issue before arriving in Mexico, and of course, if I'd known that the "white sands and warm seas" clearly depicted in their brochure and defined on their website were now off limits, we would not have taken our flippers, snorkels and face masks to Mexico. Why? Because they would have been in a suitcase most likely heading to Cyprus instead. That would have also avoided another small annoyance that you will read of shortly. There is absolutely no doubt that had we known that at times the smell from the beach was similar to the aromas that can be experienced in the British countryside when farmers are 'muck-spreading,' we would not have been at this Sensatori resort in Mexico.

So, TUI has stated that they will let us know if there is a major change that might "affect your Holiday" as soon as they can. How could they possibly have known about the naturally occurring seaweed explosion? Well I now quickly discovered that seaweed has been a major problem along the Riviera Maya coast for over six years. Yes, for over six years TUI will have known that they might not be able to offer the "White Sands and Warm Waters" that their advertising for this resort puts front and centre in their brochure and on their website. Doesn't not being able to access White Sands and Warm Waters, which TUI headline as THE major attraction, constitute a 'major effect' on our holiday? I don't just believe this to be the case, we actually experienced it.

And as well as TUI's stated commitment to us, let's not forget consumer law. The seaweed blight that affected our holiday, and thousands of others, was perfectly predictable and, under the **Package Travel, Package Holidays and Package Tours Regulations 1992**, where there are any changes to that advertised, they must be provided to the customer as soon as possible. When these elements are not followed, the customer is entitled to redress.

So, although a natural occurrence, the seaweed problem in Mexico was not unforeseen, not a chance occurrence and our disappointment was perfectly avoidable if this had been communicated to us by TUI. It has been an increasing problem since 2011 and major initiatives funded by the Mexican government are now attempting in different ways to find solutions to remove the seaweed and restore the white sands, the loss of which are adversely affecting their important tourist industry.

How did I now know this before we left Mexico?

We hadn't referenced TripAdvisor in advance of our holiday. We all know that things can go wrong, and what for one person is unacceptable, for another person the same identical situation is perfectly satisfactory. We've stayed at some places – both Sensatori and others – where everything has been excellent, and yet there are terrible reviews from people with different expectations, standards or who were travelling at different times. As was the reality for the multiple sets of transitory American neighbours in the adjacent rooms at Sensatori. Sensatori resorts are run on behalf of TUI by independent hotel companies, and in Mexico that company is Karisma Hotels. We'd had a good year and upgraded to a swim-up room in the 'Premium Section' which was next to the adults-only pool. In the Premium Section, Sensatori travellers were in a very small minority. The majority being Karisma members from the USA and Mexico. A bit like a timeshare, it seems that they pay an annual membership, and have a range of resorts they can choose to stay at. In addition to staying in the premium rooms, they get butlers who book dinner, excursions and make sure that their in-room bars are well stocked with premium-brand spirits. We found out from some of these people, in conversation as we shared swim-up pools and patio drinks, that the seaweed had been affecting this resort for many years. But unlike our two-week long-haul holiday, these Americans and Mexicans mostly came for 3-5 days, enjoyed a blitz of sunshine, fine dining and spa pampering, before a comparatively short flight home.

Then there were the weddings, more weddings and the Karisma all-day pool parties in the adults-only pool right by our room, none of which fuelled our senses!

Karisma's own website makes no mention of Sensatori visitors, nor therefore of them expecting the peace and tranquillity associated with refuelling the senses that TUI builds its Sensatori brand around.

At the time I hosted my website in October 2018, Karisma had the following image on their website, which I took a photo of.

In January 2019, it was no longer there.
(Photo of Karisma Website © Duncan Peberdy taken on 08.10.2018)

*Oops - where are the wheelbarrows and tractor?
How very careless not to include them, you might think they are trying to create a false impression - perhaps one of white sands and warm seas that can actually be enjoyed?*

Many American visitors, along with their family and friends, fly down to get married in Mexico's sunshine. Most afternoons there was a beach ceremony, sometimes two, followed by open-air receptions with a mix of lively Mexican Mariachi fused with DJ beats that continued into the evening's darkness. Great if you're the happy couple or one of their guests! Not so great if you're in the Premium accommodation block and can't escape from it. Ironically, had we not upgraded, there was a good chance we could have been located on the opposite side of the resort. But we weren't and we were on a Sensatori holiday to refuel our senses that we'd paid excellent amounts of money to enjoy. There had been several weddings at the Sensatori in Cyprus, which took place in a small Chapel outside of the hotel, and mostly between guests as part of their Sensatori holiday. They had no adverse impact on the enjoyment of others.

Alongside our 'Premium' accommodation block was the adults-only swim-up bar. It hosted the Karisma all-day pool parties. They didn't happen every day; twice during our stay in fact, when out came the Ibiza-performance speakers that played full-volume club music all day – hence the all-day pool party didn't fall into any issues with the trade descriptions act! All-day high-volume pool parties, yes. Sensatori peace and tranquillity that was supposed to refuel the senses, no!

Antisocial Media

Were TUI aware of the seaweed problems and the incompatibility between some of the Karisma events and the values of the Sensatori holiday we had been sold?

Now that I looked for supporting evidence, it wasn't difficult to find, and TripAdvisor had plenty of customer feedback. Maybe TUI purposely chooses not to look at TripAdvisor comments?

From my research I now know that the content of 'Review Portals' such as TripAdvisor was the subject of a TUI Live PolicyLounge debate that took place at TUI's Berlin Office on 29th September 2016, which was attended by Thomas Ellerbeck, a member of TUI's Group Executive Committee.

> Ellerbeck emphasised that TUI takes a very positive and proactive approach to customer feedback: "We're always delighted to receive positive feedback, and negative feedback helps us to correct our mistakes and continue improving our products."

Ellerbeck suggested that TUI should trust consumers and the internet's self-regulatory mechanisms. TUI is committed to transparency in corporate communications, political activities and travel products. This transparency strengthens the consumer's position and encourages competitors to raise their quality benchmarks.

Source: https://www.politiklounge.com/en/lounge-live/2016/2016-09-29

What sort of comments had both TUI's Sensatori and Karisma's own customers made about their Mexican resort vacation?

These were all made in advance of our holiday. Do you think that TUI had enough notice and enough time to have given us the option of enjoying a different holiday location? There are hundreds of negative comments; here is a small selection that were harvested from the TripAdvisor website in October 2018. And let's not overlook the fact that TUI have dozens of staff in resorts all along the Riviera Maya coast.

Don't forget too about the headline that was still on the Sensatori Mexico website in February 2019, where TUI continued to pedal "that the beach and sea is one of the biggest draws for this resort."

June 2017	TripAdvisor Member Sunshine720942 The beach kind of sucks too because there is seaweed everywhere. It is the worse I've ever seen. Way worse than the Dominican.
Sept. 2017	TripAdvisor Member: Lee M The seaweed on the beach is horrendous, despite efforts to keep it clear.
Oct. 2017	TripAdvisor Member Diana O – High Wycombe UK Beach was full of seaweed.
Nov. 2017	TripAdvisor Member: el2778 – Troy, USA The beach is terrible. You can expect murky water and tons of seaweed. You cannot even walk out further into the ocean without encountering seaweed
Jan. 2018	TripAdvisor Member: Corishmen_10 0 Newquay, UK Meant to be a Sensatori hotel but wasn't expecting foam parties in the pool
Feb. 2018	TripAdvisor Member: Amberleigh – Wisconsin, USA Beach is bad news. I thought I didn't mind it being rocky & not swimming- I did not anticipate the deluge of seaweed making it stinky and unattractive. They have a team of workers from sun up to sun set trying to tackle the issue one wheelbarrow at a time-but it was an impossible feat. Hotel is SMALL and LOUD, you can't get away from the noise and action. From 8am until 11pm there is constant noise. Bars, restaurant, coffee shop, beach are all blaring music nonstop. From our patio we were bombarded with the bar and coffee shops music- both playing different things at the same time. At night from 8-11p there are LOUD performances. If you're traveling with a child that goes to be before 11p- you're in trouble. There are no quiet corners to enjoy any peace.

Feb. 2018	TripAdvisor Member: Jon D – Maidenhead, UK Seaweed – There is SO much seaweed. They have workers trying to clear it all day in a completely illogical way. They use tractors for some of it but then there are these men who walk back and forth all day raking it. Sometimes taking it away, sometimes just raking it and throwing it back in the sea
March 2018	TripAdvisor Member: Joyce S And worst of all: the beach is inaccessible due to the enormous lumps of seaweed on the shore!!!!! Seriously I regret coming here! Don't come here, don't waste your money.
March 2018	TripAdvisor Member: John and Mal S – Manchester, UK The beach is like a building site; army of workers with wheelbarrows/rakes and forks trying to clear seaweed which is continually arriving on the beach. Large slicks of seaweed can be seen offshore. Also assisting the workers are a Dumper truck used as a bulldozer and a very large Tractor pulling a large scarifier.
April 2018	TripAdvisor Member: Gordon T Then there is the seaweed to contend with on the beach you have to wade through about 25feet of seaweed to get any clear water, it smells there are about 5 guys trying to clear it all with wheelbarrows and a small bobcat running up and down the beach whilst you are trying to sunbathe this problem has been going on for quite some time As I said the staff are brilliant the hotel is ok the food is good my gripe is with TUI if they had told us about the beach we would have booked a different holiday not happy ☹ put a dampener on our anniversary
April 2018	TripAdvisor Member: Clare M The red flag flew every one of the 14 day's we were at the Tui Sensatori, so if the sea is your thing then a major no go.

	Seaweed every day, some days very big heaps and to be fair the twelve labourers, one tractor and one bobcat tried valiantly to clear it every day, but it was relentless and if you google it, it has been since 2014. So for beech/sea lovers the Tui Sensatori on the East coast of the Yucatan peninsula is not a good location.
April 2018	TripAdvisor Member: DollyJan - Chester, UK If you are looking for beach holiday, then the beach here is very unusable as it has smelly rotting seaweed everywhere.
April 2018	TripAdvisor Member: sgregory189 – Kent, UK TUI should start telling the truth about the state of the sea and the beach there is so much seaweed in the sea you cannot swim in it ,all day there are tractors driving up and clearing the piles of stinking seaweed from sand and as for crystal clear water the Thames looks more inviting.
May 2018	TripAdvisor Member: John M The beach, if your expecting golden beaches DONT come to this hotel it's just seaweed with dead fish washed up in it day after day the poor guys try to clear it away but often dont make a dent in it, red flags for no swimming every day we were there
May 2018	TripAdvisor Member: Matthew F When booking a Sensatori Resort through TUI, you expect the signature high standards, beautiful resorts and a relaxing time. For this holiday, it felt short of the standards I expect from the brand. The team are fighting a losing battle with the seaweed which if you love the beach, will impact your stay, it's pretty grim.

June 2018	TripAdvisor Member: Sarah L – Froome, UK Seaweed a big problem we go for the sea/beach experience we feel we should have been told by travel agent and will be complaining as we should have been given a choice. The smell was awful at times. We know that it is nature, but we were told by a Mexican travel rep this has been problem for last 4 years
June 2018	TripAdvisor Member: Alex 10003 – Aberdeen, UK We have chosen Mexico mainly for beautiful beach and the amount of seaweed was shocking and the smell of it around the hotel. Not being able to use beach and snorkelling according to staff that outgoing issue but Tui not taking responsibility for the state of the beach. If we knew about the problem we would never go to this resort.
June 2018	TripAdvisor Member: Ptowell – Caerphilly, UK The beach was an overwhelming disappointment and I've written a complaint to TUI having discovered on arrival at the resort, that the seaweed was a known issue since at least March. I know this is a natural occurrence, but I feel we should have had notice, having been told about some minor re-tiling work that was taking place in the 2 weeks before we left. Not being able to use the beach and snorkel at the resort was a huge disappointment. We've had some fantastic holidays at other beach resorts, including Cuba, and we simply didn't consider that we wouldn't be able to snorkel or enjoy the beach and sea at a resort such as this. We knew nothing of this issue.

TUI's Company Protection Unit

On our return from Mexico I wrote to TUI with my grievances. The main ones were:

- Inaccessible beach and sea.
- Resort values not compatible as a Sensatori destination.

There were some minor irritations that might not have been worthy of a complaint in isolation, but now worth pointing out. These were:

- Excess baggage scam at Cancun airport.
- Dress Code not being upheld – again, not in line with Sensatori values personally experienced elsewhere on every other Sensatori occasion.
- Food poisoning.
- Description of excursions.

TUI provide a complaint mechanism that allows you to upload your letter with an expectation of a response within 28 days. That reply from TUI was of course late and acknowledged each of my points with a consistency of statement.

Regarding the noisy weddings:

> "These are privately arranged events and therefore we would have no control over this."

Regarding the Seaweed:

> "However, I would like to inform you that this may happen due to natural calamity and TUI is unable to have much influence over it. However, it is to be taken care by local government and the hoteliers themselves. Please be assured I am passing on my strong feedback to our resort office so that necessary feedback can be shared with the hotelier for future improvement."

Regarding the dress code:

Long trousers and no football shirts should have been the norm:

> *"I do apologise for the stress and disappointment it has caused to you. However, I would like to assure will definitely forward your strong feedback with the relevant team so that necessary changes are been made to avoid this from happening in future."*

Regarding the Excess Baggage Scam:

At the TUI check-in desk at Cancun airport, we were not able to see the weight of the baggage as the readout was only visible to the operative. We were a combined 2Kg overweight on our outbound flight (which did not cause any excess payment in Manchester), but now this had mysteriously risen to 4Kg overweight at Cancun and a $100 charge. When we got home, our digital scales confirmed we were still only 2Kg over. Now you know why I wished we had not taken two unused sets of snorkels, flippers and facemasks to Mexico!

> *"To let you know further the baggage handling done at the airport is totally under the discretion of the airport authorities and TUI is unable to have much influence over it. However, I would like to assure you will definitely share your comments with the relevant team. We will really try to take your comments on board to improve our service."*

Duh. I pointed out that the people checking-in our baggage wore TUI uniforms. The weight of baggage is surely only of consequence to TUI airlines, not the airport? You do have control. Absolute control. There was no recognition here that we were amongst the small group of TUI customers who had paid a considerable fee to upgrade to their Premium section of the Dreamliner flight. It wasn't only the seaweed that stank, TUI's attitude at Cancun airport stank too.

Regarding TUI Excursions

The first morning in resort is when the "TUI Welcome Talk" takes place and all the various excursions are offered. At this point, we hadn't discovered the full extent of the 'seaweed problem' and the excursions we booked were focused on the ancient Mayan culture, with one 'swimming with turtles' trip too. We hadn't realised – because it wasn't explicitly explained - that these trips had an average of two hours transfer time there and two hours back! There was also a trip – about an hour away we later learnt – to the 'Iles de Mejeura' – an island just off the coast by Cancun. Because the island has beaches on both sides, the sea currents don't deposit seaweed on one side of the island, leaving the 'white sand and crystal-clear waters' we were expecting at our own resort. Labour and the cost of living in Mexico is incredibly cheap by our UK standards. If TUI had organised say two complimentary trips to these islands - one each week - where we could have had the ocean experience we were sold, then that would have showed some commitment to the TUI mantra – remember, they claim to put 'U' in the middle. That would not have cost TUI a lot of money and would have demonstrated a moral commitment to providing their customers with a great holiday experience by going the extra mile.

Regarding Incompatible Karisma and Sensatori Values

Sensatori provides a great choice of restaurants for dinner each evening. No system for booking reservations is perfect and at other Sensatori resorts you book for your desired restaurant and time slot using a computer-based system up to 48 hours in advance. At the Mexico Sensatori you just turn up and if there is no immediate availability, you get given a bleeper to tell you when your table is ready; throughout our stay the waiting time was averaging about 45 minutes. If you play the game and go 45 minutes before you actually want to eat, you get straight in!

Waiting 45 minutes was not a problem, there were plenty of bars to enjoy a drink with bleeper in hand.

However, if on the other hand you were a Karisma resorts member coming in for just a few days, part of your 'deal' was that your personal butler could book any restaurant at the time of your choice. I'm sure that it wasn't beyond the wit of someone in resort to have offered this small additional convenience to TUI's loyal Sensatori customers, and again it would have just displayed some additional commitment to customers as compensation for the seaweed fiasco.

In effect, TUI had not rejected any of my complaints, they had just made a clear choice not to take any action to compensate me. They knew from my letter that I had previously been on multiple Sensatori holidays, sometimes with just my wife, at other times with both our grown-up children and their partners, and even with my parents. We are loyal TUI and Sensatori customers and this didn't seem to count for anything. Getting nowhere with my correspondence and replies from TUI's After Travel Customer Support team's own complaint procedure, it was time for a website – www.mysensatoriexperience.co.uk

On 30th October 2018 I sent another email escalating my dissatisfaction to the Managing Director of TUI UK, copying in more senior people at TUI and received 'Read Receipts' as confirmation that the emails had been opened, but no response. This was despite informing them that if I didn't get a satisfactory response, I would be initiating a claim via the Money Claims Service of the HM Courts and Tribunal Service for the sum of £3,000, approximately half the cost of our holiday. If we had known about the seaweed we would have gone elsewhere, but I was trying to be reasonable and recognise that we had received some value from the holiday.

The Broken Sensatori Promise and the power of email 'read receipts'

Once again, I was able to hunt down email addresses for a range of senior managers, press contacts, etc., at TUI, both in the UK and in Germany. I called my email subject "The Broken Sensatori Promise," and in addition to generating an inbox of 'read-receipts,' four days later I also got a telephone call from someone in TUI's Swansea call centre. It was a Saturday morning, 3rd November, and we were just about to leave in a taxi to catch a train and therefore not convenient for a conversation. The lady agreed to call back on Monday morning, but on Monday the promised follow-up call didn't come. As I was leaving on the Wednesday for a week's visit to Las Vegas, I emailed TUI's UK Managing Director, from who I had already had both delivery and read receipts for my emails. I explained that yesterday's promised call hadn't happened – I didn't have a number to call them – and that I would not be available for a week if the call didn't happen today. Within 30 minutes I received a call.

I was offered a take-it-or-leave-it offer of compensation; a smaller amount if I wanted a cheque, or a larger amount of £1400 if I accepted a voucher towards another TUI holiday. Whilst I wanted considerably more than this, and in other circumstances I would have invested £85 to issue a Money Claim via the courts for the £3,000 I had initially requested, I could see the bigger picture of getting TUI to settle now. I pushed them for a nominal additional £100 if they settled now before I headed off on holiday for a week. They agreed. I enjoyed my small additional victory, but more importantly my single-issue campaigning website tactic had gained another positive outcome. Perhaps now I had enough examples against multinational companies for this to have a much wider interest and, on the suggestion of a good friend, the possibility of my poor customer service experiences becoming an interesting book.

We accepted a higher-value voucher instead of cash as we had already booked another Sensatori holiday for June 2019 – this time to our first

Turkish Sensatori. In the same way that we had already had many completely problem-free Sensatori holidays and recognised that this was not typical, TUI should also have made the same deduction. Namely, that they had all our data, our Customer Lifetime Value as loyal Sensatori customers who had no previous history of any complaining about their Sensatori experiences and TUI should have therefore given our complaint more attention and ownership.

According to the World Economic Forum that meets annually in Davos, we are already in the early stages of the Fourth Industrial Revolution, one where the adoption of machine learning and big data will be essential for companies to be successful. TUI should have made it their business to know how valuable I have been as a customer over almost 30 years; not just our recent penchant for their Sensatori brand now that our children have grown up and fledged, but for the many, many Thomson holidays we've had as a family. For the last 20 years we've lived at the same address and had the same family name, we've filled in countless 'Customer Surveys' on the planes home where first Thomson, and now more recently as TUI, have elicited our personal data in return for tempting us (and every other hopeful mug who completed the survey) with vouchers towards a future holiday.

With big data and the ability to differentiate between loyal customers who specifically chose Sensatori and paid appropriately to expect a level of service as promised and previously experienced by this up-market brand, and those who instead were only interested in a highly-discounted last minute offer, TUI could have taken a different course of action; something wonderfully proactive and customer-centric instead of reactive fire-fighting.

Vision and Values

On its website, the following page documents TUI's Vision and Values:
https://www.tuigroup.com/en-en/about-us/about-tui-group/vision-values

It's not too dissimilar to the "If only everything in life was as reliable as a Volkswagen" promise that you will read shortly in Experience 4, and which, in my opinion, VW failed wholeheartedly to live up to.

Under the "Trusted" statement is a promise to be 'Reliable' with 'Consistent Quality.'

Clearly, and in many aspects, TUI's Mexico Sensatori fails to provide the consistent expected quality my wife and I have personally experienced at the many other Sensatori locations we have enjoyed tremendous holidays at.

Now for some personal opinions

Everything in my letters and on my website was 100% factual – no supposition, innuendo, or embellishment.

Should TUI have let the situation come to this, and have they learnt anything that will benefit customers moving forward?

On 6th November 2018 when I accepted a TUI voucher for £1500 as compensation, I mentioned to the call centre employee that the "White Sands and Warm Seas" was still being advertised on the TUI website for their Mexican Sensatori. She assured me that the 'web team' were going to change this.

Although the words 'white sands' have now been omitted, on 9th March 2019 that statement still remained front and centre promoting the resort on TUI's website.

In addition to their legal obligation under the 1992 Package Travel, Package Holidays and Package Tours Regulations, I believe that TUI, like all the companies that I've campaigned against, also have a moral obligation to their customers to provide the goods and services advertised. This means proper customer service and not adopting a default position of 'company protection at all costs' where cases are genuine. If you have made a mistake, apologise immediately, and in a manner that conveys you really mean it.

What about giving employees the authority to solve genuine customer problems – but equally to defend yourselves when a complaint is genuinely not of your making. You'll have happy customers and happy employees. This is another situation where the "Your mother would be ashamed of you" test applies. Don't have employees operating outside of a moral vacuum – there's no job satisfaction in that.

Whilst I'd like to say try not to take bad reviews personally, a little more thought, honesty and conviction towards your customers who have been genuinely let down, will remove the need for any bad reviews in the first place.

Sensatori in Turkey, at their brand-new adults-only Residence concept, was excellent.

As a footnote after looking through the few TripAdvisor reviews that I have posted, I discovered this one from 2015 after we had thoroughly enjoyed a great Sensatori stay in Cyprus.

TripAdvisor

Fantastic Sensatori Experience - again
Review of TUI Sensatori Resort Atlantica Aphrodite Hills

21.09.2015 by Duncan Peberdy

Typical of a Sensatori resort (this is our third different Sensatori destination), you can join in with everything or nothing. Rooms are a high standard; a swim-up pool lets you escape the sunbed-bingo of the main pools – although we never had any problem finding sunbeds. The buffet restaurant choice is extensive. Three themed restaurants provide a great variety. All the staff are helpful, efficient and always have a smile and 'hello'. Choice and quality of food and drink are great (except house white; average); freshly made cocktails served as the sun disappears into the sea. Entertainment is high quality; whether a guest artist or the in-house team – each of whom can hold their own on a stage. Hotel shuttles can take you to either their private beach, or a beach-club 15 minutes along the coast. Next to the hotel, the Village Square has restaurants, pub with Sky, Costa coffee, Haagen Dazs ice cream, beer garden – prices are reasonable. The Spa and Golf are located here.

If you have a problem with the Sensatori hotel at Aphrodite Hills, then take a good hard look in the mirror and you will see both the problem and the solution. You.

How to turn the standard 'no' into compensation

- Know your rights – and spend time reading the small print.
- Refer to misleading advertising claims and brand promises in your communications.
- Don't accept the first response if you're still unhappy with it.
- Use email effectively – see Chapter Six on effective use of emails for complaints.
- Don't be afraid to explain your value as a customer to the brand.
- Keep your comments factual, support them with evidence, and avoid getting emotional.
- If you're building a website, follow our simple guide included as Chapter Seven, and stick to the principles for success.

Experience Three

The Gateaux from the Chateau
but alas no "Fallen Madonna with the Big Boobies!"

A comedy of customer service errors by a local prestige venue rectified with a customised website – and a cherry on top

Set amongst rolling Worcestershire countryside and more specifically within beautiful landscaped gardens on each side of the meandering and diminutive River Salwarpe, Impney Manor - a mock Louis XIII French Chateau - was built in the eighteenth century for the Droitwich 'Salt King' John Corbett in an attempt to make his wife less homesick for the Parisian culture of her upbringing.

Photo © Duncan Peberdy

Impney Manor failed to please his wife, and after John Corbett died in 1901 the house had a succession of owners, including a brief spell as a hotel after World War 1, before being requisitioned by the War Office throughout World War 2. In 1949, after major restoration and modernisation, the property was renamed Chateau Impney and quickly became established as one of the leading hotels in the area; home of the first disco in the West Midlands, the host of 'all-nighters,' and venue for one of the earliest rock festivals in the UK, where Fleetwood Mac and Joe Cocker were headline acts. Throughout the 50s and 60s the grounds hosted many Hill Climb speed trials, which made a successful return to Chateau Impney in 2015.

It wasn't only Mademoiselle Corbett who said 'non.'

Despite its close proximity to my home, for me Chateau Impney isn't an everyday venue; it's somewhere special, a destination in its own right. The Grand Ballroom that overlooks the parkland has glamour in spades and oozes sophistication. Summer balls, Christmas Parties and wedding breakfasts have all benefitted from that certain *Je ne sais quoi*, as do the Sunday Carvery meals that take place there.   You can't argue with the Chateau's own description – *'Make your Sunday even more special with a delicious carvery in the breath-taking Grand Ballroom.'*

Well, the Sunday Carvery that I booked in the Grand Ballroom did more than just take my breath away, it left me completely and utterly gobsmacked, embarrassed for myself and my guests, and it certainly wasn't *formidable*. And you've almost certainly realised by reading this far that it wasn't the fact that things went very wrong on the day, but the way in which the management at the Chateau didn't deal with it that led to a letter of complaint, that led to an exchange of emails, that led to a website to promote the unacceptable level of customer care that I had experienced. All of which could have been avoided with a little bit of bonhomie.

Here's the "Once upon a Time" bit.

Some very good friends of my parents had recently celebrated their 60th Wedding Anniversary with a small party where guests were instructed not to bring gifts. As my parents' oldest surviving friends, I've known Barbara and Brian all my life; they were present at my wedding and I still see them every year when they make the 75-mile drive to visit my parents.   In August 2017, which was the next time that Barbara and Brian were visiting my parents, I had arranged for the six of us to enjoy the delicious Sunday Carvery in the Ballroom. I had telephoned and booked it several weeks beforehand – purposely checking that the breath-taking ballroom carvery was taking place as it can be Top-Trumped by wedding receptions and other events – and just nine days beforehand, when my wife and I were enjoying a Champagne Afternoon Tea at the Chateau (itself a gift for our own 30th Wedding Anniversary), I confirmed our Sunday Carvery booking in person with the hotel's reception team. Everything was in order. I was assured. Nine days later it certainly wasn't 'all in order.'

Despite being a very hot August Sunday, anticipating their magnificent carvery lunch in breath-taking surroundings, my guests, as is customary for many octogenarians, were uncomfortably dressed up to the nines in honour of the occasion and the location. We entered the lobby, bounded up a few stairs (well at least I did) that themselves created a feeling of expectation of good things to come, and peaked into the Grand Ballroom. It looked fantastic, just what you would expect of a room with magnificent décor, chandeliers a plenty, and ornate candlesticks on every table clearly set out for an imminent Wedding Breakfast!

I retraced my steps back to the lobby and enquired at reception about my booking for the Sunday Carvery in the Grand Ballroom. "There is no carvery today. There should have been a wedding, but it was cancelled this morning at short notice." I requested the immediate attention of the manager who arrived promptly and repeated the same information. "But I have a booking made by telephone, confirmed by email and verified here in person just nine days ago. Nobody contacted me to say that the Grand Ballroom Carvery wasn't going ahead today."

There was no 'pardon,' no sorry as if she meant it, just a dismissive and disinterested 'I'm sorry but there's nothing I can do' and a matter-of-fact alternative of Sunday Lunch in the basement restaurant should we wish to eat there instead. Now, if it had just been my wife and I, either on our own or with family and friends not in their 80s, we would have left and taken our patronage elsewhere. Not such a viable option with the responsibility of a small flock of octogenarians, so we opted for the soulless basement restaurant. To be fair, the meal was perfectly acceptable, the windowless restaurant was an escape from the heat of the day, but it wasn't the Grand Ballroom occasion that we were all dressed for and had anticipated for weeks, and not a location in keeping with the significant occasion being celebrated.

You Can't Put A Cost on It

Well you can. My parents together with their best friends were my guests, and at the end of the meal I just brandished my credit card. Still fuming about the lack of Grand Ballroom Carvery, still fuming from the lack of any concern or customer care – yep, we weren't even offered a glass of wine by way of an apology – I mistakenly paid the bill without checking it properly. The Grand Ballroom comes at a cost, and I guess that I had an expectation of what the outlay for Sunday lunch was going to be. When we got home my wife checked the bill and discovered that we had been charged the more expensive cost of a restaurant evening meal instead of the Sunday Lunch set-price deal, an overpayment of £30.00.

Whilst we are referencing sitcoms from years gone by, as Baldrick might have said, I was now "more angry than an angry thing," and drafted a complaint about the Sunday Grand Carvery fiasco (or calamite) and the overpayment, which I acknowledged that I should have checked (more) thoroughly at the time of payment. So cross was I, that I bashed out an email of complaint and sent it to the hotel's manager who responded immediately with an 'Out of Office' message informing me that he was on holiday and not returning for a further ten days. The following morning, I took my hand-delivered letter of complaint direct to the hotel.

Thank You; Perfectly Acceptable

My letter was promptly dealt with and two outcomes quickly offered and accepted. Firstly, the restaurant overpayment was acknowledged and immediately refunded. Secondly, we were offered a 50% discount on a future Grand Ballroom Sunday Carvery for the six of us, which could be taken at any time in the next six months.

Six Months, but not a day longer……

Over the winter of 2017, ill health and bad weather conspired to keep Barbara and Brian from driving to visit my parents, and it was April 2018 – some eight months after the original Carverygate fiasco – before we were ready to reschedule our celebration meal. As instructed, I contacted the Hotel Manager's PA to arrange our discounted visit, but it transpired that the previous PA had left and the new one knew nothing about the arrangement. I sent her a PDF of the letter confirming the arrangement so that the offer could be honoured. Expecting the helpful oiling of wheels to organise our booking, instead I was stopped in my tracks by the refusal of the Chateau Impney Hotel to honour the discounted meal as the six months originally stipulated had now expired.

When I contacted the Chateau to make our new booking, I had explained that we had not been able to arrange this sooner due to the illness of very old people over the winter. I now pointed out that even with a 50% discount I assumed that the Chateau would still be making money on the food, plus there was money on drinks and wine to be made. Then the small matter of restoring their reputation with local customers, not just me. I pointed out that together with different sets of friends, in recent years I've been to several Christmas Balls, the summer Gatsby Ball, and taken their summer *Tapas on the Terrace* on many occasions.

I had also purchased a full-priced Sunday Lunch for six on the day we were supposed to have experienced the Grand Ballroom. The implications of not honouring the discounted Sunday Carvery in the Grand Ballroom would impact my future custom and that of the friends, neighbours, and acquaintances I promised to educate about the poor customer service I was experiencing. The Chateau stood firm; **"Listen carefully, I will say this only once: NO DISCOUNT!"** But they did generously offer to facilitate a full-priced Grand Ballroom Carvery reservation for me. Merde.

I contacted the General Manager's PA one further time. The General Manager had been copied on this and my previous emails, and I gave them another opportunity to reconsider their position otherwise **"I'll make sure that I spread my experience of the Chateau's customer service to as many people as possible."** They made their choice not to acquiesce to my polite demands for *justice*.

This was not about money or the need for a 50% discount in order to afford a meal. This was about a point of principle following two examples of poor customer service from a business that promotes itself as the purveyors of great dining, wedding, conference, and Hill Climb experiences. It was about failing to honour an obligation to provide us with the Sunday Carvery in the Grand Ballroom experience that was outside the original six-month window because of illness to people in their 80s. I suggested that this agreement was not going to cost the Chateau, because even with a 50% discount they would still be covering their costs.

Companies House with a bit of nous!

Companies in the UK must register their business and information relating to it, such as annual accounts, directors, people with significant control, etc., all of which is available in the public domain for free at https://www.gov.uk/government/organisations/companies-house. Or just type 'companies house' into Google and follow the links. The information that could be of use isn't always obvious, so you need to know what you are looking for. For example, searching for Chateau Impney won't find the information you want because it's not the official name of the company behind it.

Most websites have a 'legal' or 'privacy' link; not always obvious but usually somewhere at the bottom of the page, and the Privacy Notice on the Chateau Impney website tells you that Greyfort Hotels Limited is responsible for the Chateau Impney website, and a quick Companies House search instantly reveals that Greyfort Hotels, Greyfort Properties, Greyfort Finance and Greyfort Investments are all companies using the Chateau Impney as their official address. Searching these companies on the Companies House website discloses the names of the people with significant control, from which searches to find emails addresses for them can be made.

Fans of the 80s UK Sitcom *'Allo 'Allo!* will understand my 'Gateaux from the Chateau' silliness, but the website I created - www.mychateauimpneyexperience.co.uk - had no such humour.   Instead it just listed the facts about the original debacle in August 2017 and the position that the Chateau took some eight months later.   It also contained some factual information about the financial position of the company, based on the latest set of accounts filed on the Companies House website which are available to anyone with an interest and internet access.

If you remember that after declining to honour the future discount for a second time, I promised the Chateau's General Manager and his PA that *"I'll make sure that I spread the Chateau's position on customer service to as many people as possible."*   My website did just that, and in informing both of these people of the website's presence and a link to it, I was able to copy a Director of Greyfort Hotels Limited, who's email address I'd now found, on the distribution.

Light Blue Touch Paper – Do Not Return if Ignition Fails. Ignition did NOT fail.

The domain name – www.mychateauimpneyexperience.co.uk had cost me £2. There was no cost for hosting the website as I was able to create this as a sub-domain off another site already being hosted. To put the information together in an attractive looking way took a few hours of my time.

Complaining just for complaining sake is not the way I work. Every restaurant or business can have an off-day, and if they put it right that is the end of the matter. Obviously, the Chateau was not aware that I had discovered a tried and tested way of publicly stating my point of view that had proven successful on previous occasions. Until today.

At 14.44 on Friday 20th April 2018 I sent my email. Within two hours I received a phone-call from the Director at Greyfort Hotels Limited whom I had copied into the email, wanting to discuss the content and intention of my website. He asked why I had not contacted him personally before to discuss this. I responded that he employs a General Manager who himself has a Personal Assistant, and I ventured that there must be something wrong with their management system if neither the General Manager nor the Personal Assistant are empowered to sort out a complaint that would – I again explained – not actually cost the business any cold hard cash!

This was a new situation for me. Firstly, all the other companies that had not satisfactorily responded to letters and email and which resulted in a complaining website, were multinational companies. The Chateau was a local and a comparatively small company. Secondly, people, who might be searching for information on the Chateau and then stumble across my website, could well be people that I know. This local element was the focus of the Director's objection to my website. In his opinion, there was the chance that the Chateau would lose business as a result, jeopardising the employment of local people and suppliers to the hotel. So, whilst he clearly wanted the website taken down immediately, he also recognised explicitly the need to sort out a suitable way forward with me that provided the customer service I had been seeking in the first place, in order to make that happen.

Let's Do *Tapas on The Terrace*

Unfortunately, the failing health of my octogenarian friends meant that they were unlikely to visit Droitwich again soon, so I didn't want a carvery for six people at any price. It had been many years since I'd last had a Chateau carvery, and a scrumptious as I remembered it, the prospect of another one currently left a bad taste in my mouth. On the other hand, one of our guilty pleasures and indulgences during the last few years has been enjoying *Tapas on the Terrace* at the Chateau on warm summer evenings. A selection of authentic Spanish Tapas with some draught Spanish lager and Italian Prosecco; what's not to like?

After a bit of horse-trading we agreed on the following deal to bring matters to a close. I would enjoy *Tapas on the Terrace* for six people, for which I would only pay 25% of whatever the actual bill came to. That, I was told, reflected the cost of the food and would incur the Chateau a loss on whatever alcohol we had. As testament to the type of person that I really am, I said that our evening would not abuse the situation. In other words, the people that I took to the Chateau would not be aware of the arrangement, so that expensive champagne or other liberties would not be taken. And that's exactly what happened. Within five minutes the website was removed from public view, and a few short months later six of us enjoyed a fabulous sunshine evening on the terrace with our Spanish Tapas, Spanish Lager and Italian Prosecco. (Yes – indeed where was the Spanish Cava?) And being true to my word, it was only after I'd settled the bill and generously tipped the highly attentive staff for their impeccable service, that I explained to my guests why I was paying the bill.

Needless to say, in my opinion the remedy from the Chateau only came about because there was the prospect of being publicly shamed and because only now did they value their reputation. This wasn't the case when they originally embarrassed me with my guests, nor when they chose not to honour their offer to put things right because it was outside of the original six months. When the deal was agreed for me and my guests to enjoy *Tapas on the Terrace*, it was implied that the Chateau's cost of food is generally 25% of the retail price, which confirms my earlier assumption that at a 50% discount they would still have been making money on the Carvery meals.

I do have mixed feelings about using my website tactic with smaller local businesses. But on the other hand, these are typically owner-managed businesses that need to have a much better handle on customer service and dealing with complaints; with social media and local word of mouth, negative publicity can damage their own business potential almost in the blink of an eye. Where the responsibility for customer service is in the hands of employees, so should the empowerment to quickly rectify a situation that can lead to unforeseen knock-on consequences if not dealt with in this way.

And let's also not lose sight of the fact that not once have I deliberately engineered any opportunity to put information so quickly about my experiences into the public domain. It has always been only after the company in question has had numerous opportunities to redress the situation of the complaint but, like the management at the Chateau Impney, has itself chosen not to do so.

Learnings:

I still believe that the Chateau provided me and my friends with *Tapas on The Terrace* not because they felt their initial customer service to me personally warranted it (they had, after all, already rejected opportunities to do so previously), but because they needed a resolution to a customer service situation that now had the possibility to be more widely known, and they recognised the potential negative (local) publicity it could generate. Resolving **CarveryGate** at the time would not have cost them any loss of earnings, whereas our *Tapas on the Terrace* drinks, though not excessive, would have been provided at a loss.

Had the Chateau Impney willingly provided the discounted Grand Ballroom Carvery, they may have enticed us into an experience that we would have repeated by now with other family and friends. We might have felt valued as a customer and returned to the summer ball and Christmas party at the Chateau, along with our friends and neighbours who spend generously on wine and at the bar at these events. For our 2018 Christmas party we went instead to Worcester Rugby Club, and for Christmas 2019 we booked inexpensive flights to Amsterdam, visited the floating Christmas market and enjoyed a great meal and weekend in the beautiful city of Leiden. We never returned for *Tapas on the Terrace* – we've found an alternative that isn't quite as glamorous, but which suits our mindset more fully – nor any other Summer Balls and the like.

COVID-19 and beyond...

Since early April 2020 the Chateau Impney has been the talk of the town for all the wrong reasons. Following the Government order on Friday 20th March for hotels, pubs and restaurants to close in response to the COVID-19 pandemic, on 3rd April news broke that the Chateau had decided to close for good.

Everyone locally seems to have their own "Well I'm not surprised" story about poor customer service and how for the last ten years plus the Chateau has not appeared in their own minds to have realised its *'great potential.'*

IF the Chateau Impney reopens under genuinely new ownership, I will be very happy to try once more to give it a fresh opportunity to claim our regular custom.

Tackling smaller local companies who fail to deliver

- It's not only big companies you take on with a customised website. The tactic works for businesses of all sizes - with social media and local word of mouth, negative publicity can damage their own business potential almost in the blink of an eye.
- I have found most small businesses will go out of their way to avoid a negative complaint posted online – but remember to do this when you have a genuine complaint, not as a threat to get a discount or freebie.
- Give the business reasonable time to respond to your grievances before resorting to a website – it should not be your first reaction.
- As with all the examples in this book, keep a diary of your complaint and keep all correspondence in one place in case you need it.
- If the company you are complaining about is privately owned, you can find out all about their ownership and financial status by looking at Companies House. This can be invaluable when composing your complaint: https://www.gov.uk/get-information-about-a-company.
- Know what you want in compensation – and be reasonable. For me, these complaints are never about the money (although that is important), they are about a principle. Be clear about your expectations of what you want with the company, and don't settle for anything less.
- Remember smaller local companies aren't usually cash rich. The *Tapas on the Terrace* is a great example of this. I also know some people who prefer a donation to a local charity.

Experience Four

Would YOU Buy a Volkswagen Tiguan?

Defying depreciation: Turning threats of legal action against me from a VW dealership into a brand-new car by using a website to promote my on-going complaint

This was the first occasion when I escalated my complaint to a public website.

After being smitten in 2006 with the gorgeous design of VW's forthcoming 4 x 4 when it was unleashed as a concept car to the world in a stunning orange livery with a supporting cast of black and orange tyres, in 2008, shortly after it had been released for sale in the UK, I found myself ordering one. Sadly, orange wasn't an option at any price, but I was very excited for my new car when I took delivery in May 2008. There were a couple of early minor niggles; a faulty CD player and the incorrect service intervals electronically selected, but for 12 months my Tiguan was undeniably the great car I anticipated it to be. It was, after all, my fourth VW having previously driven a Golf and two Passats.

If only everything in life was as reliable as a Volkswagen!

But from May 2009 to March 2010 my Tiguan displayed a series of faults, some of which were production related, others because of an engine management system highlighting faults that subsequently didn't seem to exist, and others as a result of poor vehicle servicing and lacklustre customer service. Following fault after fault reported on the display by the engine management system, the only course of resolution seemed to be the hopeful resetting of the display codes. And, as we all know, 'hope' should never be a strategy for any successful outcome. Eventually I lost complete faith with the reliability of my Tiguan.

It was not just the electronic and mechanical problems with the Tiguan itself, is was also the fact that my telephone calls and letters to both VW and the local reseller were obviously not being given enough attention as for the majority of time they went unanswered. The time had come for a new and hitherto un-tested approach. With a catalogue of itemised occasions when my Tiguan had failed and itself reported dealer interventions as a matter of urgency, and with no guarantee from either VW or their authorised reseller of what would happen if these unrelated faults continued to deliver an unacceptable level of vehicle unreliability, I formally asked VW to provide me with a brand-new replacement. Not for one moment did I expect to receive a new Tiguan as compensation for the problems with my now two-year-old Tiguan.

What I really wanted was for VW to discover the underlying reason why my Tiguan kept failing, and for them to put it right, and I thought that by opening the bargaining at a high level this might force the attention needed. However, VW informed me that any decision to replace the car rested solely with the reseller, who subsequently advised me that I would have to take legal action against them if I wanted any such outcome.

Legal Action? In totally different circumstances, I've witnessed at first-hand how family members have embarked on legal action with the belief that they were 100% in the right, only for a technicality or procedural issue to thwart their claim and instead of getting the justice they felt morally entitled to, they were left with substantial legal costs of both parties to pay.

Not therefore wanting to embark on legal action, instead I created a website to air my grievances. Do bear in mind that this was in early 2010 and websites with reviews were in their infancy and none of these provided a viable option that I felt met my needs. Also, I didn't want my complaint to be just another moaning dirge amongst many unconnected complaints of varying levels. What really made a difference to my story was the reseller, the one that was unwilling to solve the problems with my continually failing car, who then reacted to a potentially embarrassing situation by unleashing their own solicitor with written threats of legal action against me.

As you will read, the upshot was that VW finally took my complaint seriously enough to offer me a trade-in value of £22,235 on a car that was now over two years old, had over 45,000 miles on the clock, and which had originally cost £24,065. Now if only every car depreciated so little over two years and 45.000 miles! The only conditions were that I had to have a brand-new Tiguan to replace it with and I had to remove my website from public access. Finally, I got the result I had been looking for all along; reliable motoring.

Not exactly 'living the dream!'

To put this story in to some context, you need to understand that I'm not really a car person, in the sense that specs and performance are not something that consume my time. What interests me about a car is really quite shallow:

- Does it look good?
- Has it got the features that will benefit me?
- Can I afford it?
- Is it a good deal?

In that case, when can I have one in the colour of my choice?

To prove my point, back in 1984 my first new car was a white 1300 MG Metro (yes, really!) because at the time I worked for the diplomatic service and there were great discounts when exporting a British car to Germany where I was about to be posted as a very junior clerical assistant at the Consulate General in Munich. In stereotypical boy-racer style on no-speed-limit German autobahns, I thrashed that first car to within an inch of its life. I found out the hard way that a 1.3 litre engine is really no match for the unlimited speeds on a German autobahn and that sooner or later your gearbox won't cope with repeated 350-mile journeys at maximum revs with autobahn acceleration and braking levels. I found out, to my considerable cost, that when you hit a deep pothole on a country road in a modestly priced car and travelling at a reasonable speed, that your car's sub-Frame is likely to twist. I didn't even know that cars had sub-Frames until I hit a deep pothole at a reasonable speed on a country road and, at a great ensuing expense, twisted mine. But when some four years later (in early 1988) I was preparing to return to the UK as a much older, wiser, and now married man with more sensible driving habits, Volkswagen were offering tax-free exports and diplomatic discounts resulting in our first order for a VW; a bright red Golf.

In the years that followed, amongst a range of no-choice company cars, the next two cars that I selected and purchased were both VW Passats and all of these cars had lived up to the VW promise of reliability. Then in 2006, VW created their first concept compact 4x4, called it a Tiguan, and when they unveiled it at the Los Angeles Auto Show the images of an orange car with orange and black tyres was very alluring and shortly after they finally went on sale in the UK, I ordered one – the only drawback for me being that an orange version with orange and black Continental tyres was not an available option.

VW's gorgeous concept car with its black and orange tyres!

The fuel consumption of my new Tiguan wasn't brilliant, but I could get almost 30,000 miles out of a set of tyres and over 20,000 miles between services. Yes, with kids in the car and a wife in the passenger seat, those boy-racer days were well and truly behind me. More importantly, the Tiguan with its elevated driving position was great to drive, and without doubt it was the best car I had ever owned and the most enjoyable to drive. Then after twelve months and with just over 30,000 miles clocked up, my Tiguan started to misbehave and become fabulously unreliable. It suffered from multiple failures over a relatively short period of time, with many of them triggering a yellow illuminated 'take me to your dealer' warning light on the instrument panel. The most frustrating situation was that in many cases the reason for the warning lights proved not to be clear, but of course when you're motoring along and the yellow warning light comes on and tells you to visit the nearest dealer, you don't wait on the off-chance that there isn't actually a problem at all.

Time and time again, and all within a relatively short period of time, my Tiguan told me that it was wanted back in the workshop. On too many occasions the precise cause of the fault couldn't be determined, and so the relevant bit of the engine management system was simply reset electronically without any actual remedy, and the problem temporarily went away. What actually went away was the warning light and error codes being reported, until the next incident came along.

To be fair to my local authorised VW dealer, and unlike BMW as you will have read earlier, they did always try to provide a courtesy car when my Tiguan was with them for more than just a few hours. On a couple of occasions, I was loaned a very sexy Passat CC belonging to the service manager that had all the bells and whistles on it, and which was a real thrill to drive for the 48 hours it was entrusted to me. I was tempted; those distant boy-racer days whispered longingly in my ear....

A pattern was now emerging. My Tiguan put up a fault symbol on the instrument panel with a 'take me to your dealer' code or instruction, I took it to the dealer, they couldn't find the source of the reported problem, so they just reset the code and gave it me back. Looking back, at least they were honest about it, but after this happened more than a dozen times, my confidence in my Tiguan quickly diminished. Frankly, I didn't want it anymore; what I really didn't want was the unreliability and the seemingly ongoing unknown reasons for it.

As well as these very real issues of unknown origin, there were physical faults with the parking brake (twice), the throttle valve, the angle cap, and the coolant pump, all of which were replaced under warranty. These other 'faults' were disturbing my confidence in VW.

I wrote to the nice people at VW UK a letter explaining exactly what was going on with my Tiguan that they had built, and politely asked them to take my car back and give me a new one as a replacement. They declined my suggestion and pointed out that my car was still under warranty and that each time it had failed, they had rectified the problem. Strictly speaking they hadn't. Yes, they had taken the car into the workshop at no physical cost to me – apart from lost time and frustration – but they hadn't solved anything as the unidentified problems just kept occurring and the same ritual was re-enacted, not unlike a Sealed Knot battle re-enactment weekend in Tewkesbury. Perhaps.

Of course, I didn't really expect them to give me a brand-new replacement car for a vehicle that was over two years old and with 45,000 miles on the clock. However, whilst they were making the warning lights go out and the 'take me to your dealer' messages go away in the short term, I didn't feel that they were taking enough ownership about a long-term remedy. How many more times would I have to be inconvenienced before they actually did something proactive rather than just all the fire-fighting? Who, just as importantly to me, should I be complaining to? My contract had been with the local authorised VW dealer from whom I had purchased my car, and yet, as I understood it, the warranty repairs were funded by VW themselves.

I was by now far more than fed up with telephone calls, letters and emails not getting anywhere, and by anywhere, I mean no real ownership to solve my problems, just a continuing reactive rear-guard. For example, because I was continuing to have problems into the third year of ownership, VW offered me an extended warranty with a 50% discount. They just didn't get it. I didn't want to manage future problems at my cost, I wanted the current ones to go away for good and they didn't have a mechanism to guarantee this.

Looking back ten years, I'm not sure where the impetus to create a website came from. I don't recall seeing anything similar. But I simply registered a pertinent domain name, in this case www.wouldyoubuyavwtiguan.co.uk, and hosted my very basic website for the world to see.

From the start I knew that the information on the site had to be factual, with no supposition, personal opinions or theories – just the facts. On the site I listed down a timeline of all the things that had gone wrong with my Tiguan; item by item, with dates and service department job numbers. There was a tab for details of correspondence, and a tab for 'direct action.' This was also a key moment in my battle with VW.

The Siege of Comet

In early 2010, and I wasn't expecting this, the Daily Mail came to my aide. They told the story of two plucky pensioners, Andrew and Jeannie Kelly, who successfully took some direct action when the love and care they were receiving from Comet in response to a broken laptop didn't live up to Comet's promises. A faulty Toshiba laptop, just over 30 days old and clearly still well within warranty, was sent back to Germany for repair with an explicit expectation of no more than 2 weeks to complete the repair and return. When they went back to collect the laptop as agreed, they eventually discovered that it was still in Germany and the repair hadn't yet started. After another 40-mile round trip and again finding their laptop was still in Germany, they requested Comet supply them with a new laptop. When that fell on deaf-ears in a 'computer-says-no' style scene from Little Britain, Mr Kelly decided it was time for 'Direct Action'. Andrew and Jeannie created their own placard headed "Con-et not Comet" and armed with coffee flasks for a cold February morning stood outside Comet in Lincoln and informed every Comet customer about their poor customer experience.   It took around two-hours, but eventually the manager appeared and was now empowered to give them there and then a replacement laptop, a 30% refund, and an upgraded warranty free of charge. Comet had been shamed into doing the right thing by some high visibility direct action.

Thanks to Andrew and Jeannie's Daily Mail story with its accompanying photo, I suggested to my local VW dealer that I would have my Tiguan sign-painted with the address of my website (www.WOULDYOUBUYAVWTIGUAN.co.uk) in big letters and park my Tiguan on the public road outside their main entrance during a Bank Holiday weekend.

Did they do the right thing? No, but they did something that greatly assisted in bringing my action against VW to an endpoint. They got their solicitor to write to me with the threat of a legal injunction if I took that direct action with MY car. They also made an offer to part-exchange my Tiguan for a new Tiguan if I were to pay £4,000. Had this been offered without all the shenanigans that had proceeded and forced it, I probably would have accepted it. But they were now doing this not because it was the right thing to do, but because I had become a nuisance as a result of their previous inactions.

It didn't help my mental health to know that the local VW dealer was prepared to pay for legal advice and the cost of having a warning letter sent to me, instead of doing the right thing for their customer with ongoing complaints over many months. It also didn't seem in keeping with their stated positions on customer service.   On the cover of the folder that contained the paperwork for my car when it was handed over to me, it states in a relatively large font designed to stand out:

> **The Listers Volkswagen Group**
>
> **Who are we?**
>
> **Established in 1979, the Listers Group now employ over 1200 people who strive to provide industry leading standards of customer satisfaction.**
>
> **Our organisation is structured to meet the ever-increasing needs of our customers, providing them with an outstanding level of customer service that encourages them to come back to Listers time and time again.**
>
> **We trust you will enjoy our unique customer focus. The key to our success is customer satisfaction and we strive to achieve excellence in every aspect of our business.**

Now before I tell you what I did next, let me just remind you that both this reseller and VW UK knew that I had previously owned a Golf and two Passats; I had actually traded-in a Passat with them when I purchased my Tiguan. Whilst threatening me with legal action if I took direct action that might negatively affect their business, in my opinion any risk of damage to their business was because between them and VW they were not dealing properly with the ongoing problems my Tiguan was suffering from. Cause and effect. If they had solved the problems with my Tiguan, by providing an acceptable level of customer service, none of this would have been necessary.

Their dalliance with a solicitor also gave me the ammunition to contact VW's UK Managing Director and inform him that a "**loyal VW customer threatened with legal action.**" My email with its concise title did the trick.

Now the CEO of VW had been the recipient of many emails from me before this. Remember this was back in 2010 when it was much easier to find email addresses for corporate leaders than it is today. I'm guessing that previous emails had been either:

- A victim of the delete key – such customer service emails are not the concern of a CEO, especially if they are copied to the company's customer service team too.
- Intercepted by the CEO's PA who will almost certainly have a duplicate of the CEO's in-box on her computer to control.
- Forwarded by the CEO or his PA to the customer service team.

But on this occasion, and within 24 hours, I received a telephone call from VW's Head of Customer Service requesting to come and meet with me personally and discuss my issues with the aim of finding a resolution. Now you dear reader can decide if VW had sprung into 'customer service' action or 'company protection' action, but as far as I was concerned, there was now the prospect of the ongoing mechanical and electrical problems with my beautiful Tiguan being remedied.

Whether it was only at this point, after the lazy threat of legal action instead of sorting out my problems, that the presence and content of my website really came onto the radar with people within VW who could bring about change I'll probably never know. But it was a lovely warm day when the lady from VW rang my door bell and we sat in the garden somewhat convivially discussing how VW now wanted to bring this on-going saga to a close.

Two great things then happened. Firstly, she apologised to me, on behalf of herself for not getting involved earlier, and on behalf of VW for the problems my Tiguan had caused. She apologised as if she meant it, and I believed she did. She wasn't a 'company protection officer,' because she also informed me that she was empowered to do 'whatever was necessary' to bring this to a close. She acknowledged and was apologetic that my Tiguan had "encountered too many different problems for a premium brand."

I just wanted to have my car in full working order. I don't know if VW wanted to have my car back to interrogate it and learn any lessons from it or simply to crush it? It's clear from the product recalls that all car manufacturers experience, that it can take some time – often many years – before a part in a car that was never expected to fail, fails. For future manufacturing the part gets replaced or modified, but for all existing drivers the car is recalled, and a free-of-charge repair performed. Or perhaps it was just one of those cars built first thing on a Monday or last thing on a Friday? I'm sure with modern automation on production lines this doesn't really happen. Perhaps the kindest way, the way to stop any future customer buying this car and having yet more problems, was to euthanise it with the big car-crusher.

"Whatever was necessary." As a salesman, this was a great buying signal that the deal was mine to be had, and I could push it quite far. Now that their CEO was involved, hopefully she wouldn't want to leave without reaching an agreement to move forward with me. "Just replace my car with a new like-for-like one at no cost to me." That was a great place to start. How do you work out what value I had enjoyed from the car before all the problems started, compared to the compensation for the poor quality of car and customer service? The dealer had originally offered me a deal that would have resulted in me paying £11,000 for a new vehicle, which with the intervention of a solicitor had been reduced to around £4,000. So "Whatever was necessary" gave me the upper hand. The horse-trading continued over a cup of tea with a chocolate hob-nob. Two years on, the exact specification of my Tiguan was no longer available as mine had been a short-term special that included some items in a combination that could not now be ordered. It was either a slightly higher-specification or a slightly-lower one, and finally we agreed on the slightly higher one which would cost me a contribution of £2,000.00 if I wanted to proceed with that as a full and final resolution, which also included my agreement, in writing, to take down my website.

The website had ultimately had an effect and I was satisfied to agree to both this and the £2,000 payment contribution towards a brand-new Tiguan in exchange for my now very unreliable one. It wasn't going to be a car that was already sat on a forecourt somewhere, but one built to the colour and specification we'd agreed, and which would take around eight weeks to materialise from the Fatherland!

When my replacement Tiguan with its gorgeous new-car smell was ready at the same local reseller, I went in with my cheque book, paid them the £2,000 and drove home happy. I was expecting a simple receipt for my £2,000.00, but instead was presented with a full sales invoice, as I had for my previous cars purchased here, with a full listing of the specification, the full retail price, minus a trade-in credit for my problem child. "Trade-In Value - £24,000."

If only everything in life was as reliable as a Volkswagen! – Revisited in 2020

Those of a certain age will remember that for many many years, VW ran a series of adverts on TV and in newspapers to educate us to the fact that above all else VW cars were reliable. "If only everything in life was as reliable as a Volkswagen."

Was this not an implicit contract of reliability that was now being broken?

This was my first example of using the internet as a vehicle (every pun intended) for getting the necessary people to notice my fully documented complaint about my Tiguan's unreliability. The necessary people being the ones with enough managerial gravitas to make something happen in the world of customer service.

When does an unconnected string of minor faults become an issue that should result in a like-for-like replacement? The problem with the car industry, unlike pretty much anything else, is that a large section of the car market is made up of second-hand cars, with the same authorised resellers involved with both sections of the market. You don't get Curry's selling second-hand TVs or washing machines, or DFS selling second-hand sofas. Also, cars depreciate in a way that none of these other products do, which makes having any policy to replace after its been driven off the forecourt very difficult to achieve. In my case, I'd had value from the car for two years, but I'd also had a load of aggravation, wasted hours of my time visiting the dealership, and experienced the constant worry of on-going unreliability. Remember VW's mantra that they should have been living up to – "if only everything in life was as reliable as a Volkswagen."

Many of the faults, like headlights, (that had nothing to do with bulbs or fuses,) exhaust systems, where warnings generated by the electronic management system even though it transpired that no actual fault existed. These didn't occur just once or twice, but multiple times each. Then there were the faulty electronic hand brake – twice, the faulty throttle valve, the faulty pressure sensor. But it was the continual fault in the exhaust system – often wrongly blamed on the Diesel Particulate Filter – although this never appeared as a separate warning in its own right and my car was not used for 'school runs and shopping' often associated with the persistent low mileage journeys that can result in Diesel Particulate Filter errors.

The 'errors in the exhaust system' were accompanied with the requirement to bring this to the dealer's attention at the earliest possible opportunity. Too many times the 'remedy' was to simply reset the error codes in the Electronic Management System as no actual fault could be found. Not an action that instils customer confidence in the reliability of their car.

I kept my replacement Tiguan for around two years. My employment circumstances changed, and I was supplied with a company car with a very large payload that could accommodate some of the sizable products the company I was now working for manufactured.

Will I buy another VW?

On reflection, my previous three VW's and my replacement Tiguan fully lived up to VW's reliability mantra. Would I buy another VW again? Well life moves on and we've had a VW emissions scandal, one that ironically affected my replacement Tiguan, so I would have to think very long and very hard about that, and the answer would probably still be no.

Defeating car dealerships

- When making a considered purchase like a car, put in writing what you want – you can always refer to this if there's a problem.
- Keep a factual diary as problems occur, list what you did, and what the supplier did
- Keep all service and repair documentation.
- Use your smartphone camera to keep a visual record of problems – useful later on if you need to create a campaigning website.
- Be clear on what is a reasonable level of faults, and what is unreasonable - like the totally unreliable Tiguan.
- Refer to the dealerships' customer charter or marketing messages in your communications to show how they are failing to meet their own promises.
- Escalate the problem to the brand owner – car dealerships are franchisees and measured constantly on metrics that include customer satisfaction and loyalty.
- Don't be intimidated by threats of legal action – in this case it gave me the upper hand to negotiate a favourable resolution.
- Start from a position of authority when settling by knowing your consumer rights

- If all else fails, build a website and promote your grievance. Read the chapter on building a website.

Footnote:
Throughout my complaint it remained unclear as to whether my resolution was for VW or the local authorised reseller to solve, especially as my sales contract and invoice was from the reseller, whilst the three-year warranty is provided by the manufacturer.

Experience Five

Getting Microsoft to "scratch beneath the Surface!"

Turned a total *'computer says NO'* roadblock into a satisfactory conclusion without the need for a website!

When I encountered a terminal technical tantrum with an almost brand-new and very expensive Microsoft Surface Pro laptop, Microsoft's service department's process was to replace my faulty expensive device with a refurbished second-hand unit rather than repair mine or replace it with a new one. Discover why I didn't believe that replacing my laptop with a refurbished unit, that had in effect already failed for someone else, was acceptable, and how I succeeded in getting the resolution I felt was justified for such a supposedly professional and expensive piece of technology.

Would you have been satisfied to receive a repaired device as a replacement for an almost-new expensive purchase? That's exactly how Microsoft expected to resolve my situation, and for me that wasn't acceptable.

It is estimated - according to my go-to research consultant of choice, Google - that over 1 billion PC's worldwide are using Microsoft's Windows operating system. Add to that the domination of Microsoft Office for word processing, spreadsheets, presentations, etc., and the popularity of Xbox in the gaming world, and you have a huge amount of Microsoft product out there. No wonder then that in late April 2019 Microsoft became only the third US $1 Trillion Dollar Company – after Apple and Amazon – and have once again become the world's most valuable company.

Now when it comes to Windows, most of the computers that have it installed are manufactured by other companies; Dell, Toshiba, HP, Acer, etc. But in 2012 Microsoft launched a small range of touchscreen computers, under the name **Surface,** that it had designed and developed and positioned in the market as aspirational purchases. Over successive years, Microsoft's Surface range has grown whilst retaining its perception of being at the 'luxury-end' of the market, with pricing that in my opinion upholds those assumptions.

Talking of luxury products, who remembers the early TV adverts for Belgium's Stella Artois lager? "Reassuringly Expensive" was the tagline for a premium drink that commanded a premium price. Stella Artois were also, for many years, sponsors of the pre-Wimbledon Queen's Club tennis tournament and another reinforcement of exclusivity with its association to London SW6. In other words, quality and cheap are not great bedfellows.

Reassuringly Expensive

When Microsoft launched their Surface Pro laptops they were also, in my opinion, reassuringly expensive. With their sleek designs and positioned as the new single solution that would replace the requirement to have a separate laptop and separate tablet (read iPad here), they were also aspirational. I wanted one. Laptop by day, iPad by evening; the first serious offering to address the keyboard and mouse needs of a business user with the no-keyboard no-mouse needs of a social tablet user. Having said that, on top of the reassuringly expensive price, Microsoft charge an additional £124.99 for a bespoke re-chargeable keyboard that also covers and protects the tablet screen when not in use, and which attaches directly to the Surface Pro for power charging and connectivity. A third-party Bluetooth keyboard might save you over £100 but will detract massively from the experience. If I was bothered about cars, getting a compatible non-Microsoft Bluetooth keyboard might be the equivalent of buying a sports car and only equipping it with re-tread tyres – I think.

Yes, I know what you're thinking and I'm with you on that. Surely, I can hear your mind's eye vocalise, when you pay a seriously good amount of money for a sparkling new device that is supposed to replace your business laptop, might you not expect it to include the keyboard as standard? Who has ever purchased a computer laptop that doesn't have a keyboard? Well, with the Microsoft Surface Pro 4 that I purchased back in 2016, and even with the swanky new Surface Pro 6 currently tempting buyers, the keyboard remains an optional extra.

Having procrastinated over the cost of my purchase for a few months, in January 2016 I decided I was worth it and ordered a Surface Pro 4 at a cost of £1568 (this included the optional keyboard, the optional pen and a docking station for my office desk). That wasn't the price for their lowest specification Surface Pro, but I really couldn't see the point of not going for one that might be more capable of remaining technologically relevant for a bit longer. So, I plumped for one at the higher end of the spec with an i7 Intel processor 64Gb of RAM, and 64-bit operating system. I might not know the specification of my cars, but when it comes to technology, I know a thing or two, and having a higher specification of machine gives it a better chance of longevity as new software releases always seem to require ever more processing power and memory to function effectively. I like to think that I've proved a point here, if only to myself. In April 2020 I was still using the same computer to type this manuscript, although the expensive keyboard or the connection to it gave up the ghost over 12 months ago and I'm now using a 're-tread' that has a separate charging cable and which I sometimes forget to re-charge. The thing is, I can't now see the point of investing £125 in a new keyboard when something different is calling; just like Leipzig in the Thomas Dolby song, my name is being called....

The day my Surface Pro 4 decided not to work

When I say that I'm still using the same computer, that's not factually true. Yes, it's the identical specification of Surface Pro 4, but after my original one failed on me, it's a different unit with a different serial number. That's exactly where the problem started, the day my original very new Surface Pro 4 decided it didn't want to work anymore.

I loved my Surface Pro 4; even before I purchased it. Nobody else that I was working with had one; a few people had the earlier versions which weren't as reassuringly expensive, and some of which had a restrictive version of Windows installed. I had the dog's nuts. Then very soon after taking delivery direct from the Microsoft on-line store it stopped working. For a couple of weeks it had worked and by now I'd transferred all my programmes, digital images and documents to it. But now, just minutes before an important presentation, it wouldn't power-up properly. Consulting Google, ironically from an iPad because my Surface Pro wasn't working! there were some documented issues around the new Surface Pro 4's not booting, together with potential remedies that required a (seemingly) endless cycle of powering off holding down buttons and then powering on holding a different button. Despite all my bold attempts with the required finger dexterity to solve the issue, I still couldn't get to the main screen and consequently no ability to work. I spoke to a Microsoft support expert who, after talking me through a series of guided diagnostic attempts to boot with various combinations of buttons pressed, released and pressed again, declared that my Surface Pro 4 needed to visit PC sick-bay back at Microsoft.

So, here's how Microsoft's warranty for their flagship Surface Pro 4 worked, or rather didn't for my particular circumstance and against my expectations. You've already heard me say that its completely unrealistic to expect everything in life to be perfect, and that it's usually when things go wrong that we better understand the companies and people we are dealing with. Because my device was just a few days outside of

Microsoft's 14-day window, where any failures would be treated as 'dead on arrival' and automatically replace with a brand-new unit, my Surface Pro 4 would now be subject to their advance exchange service (AES) warranty. My almost-new and hardly used Surface Pro would be collected after Microsoft had sent me an identically-specified refurbished unit. Initially I thought that this was just a stop-gap until MY Surface Pro was repaired and returned. But that wasn't the case at all. The refurbished device - effectively somebody else's expensive Surface laptop that had, like mine, failed and had been sent back for repair - would now be mine to keep. MY Surface Pro, once repaired, would provide the same warranty replacement for someone else.

There it was. My faulty flagship Microsoft purchase costing over £1500, less than a month old and promoted by Microsoft as "the performance solution for professionals," was now going to be replaced with a once-faulty second-hand refurbished unit. Not exactly very professional; in fact, a very rude way to treat your customers; in my opinion.

Fault Fixing: Microsoft vs Apple; there's no comparison

Microsoft were aiming their Surface Pro 4 at high-end users, people who might have been considering a MacBook Pro as an alternative.   Never mind something costing over fifteen hundred quid, let me share with you a fantastic warranty repair experience from Apple on an item costing – from memory – around £200.

Who can remember a time when the first iPods were on the market and required you to connect a cable to your PC, insert your music CD's and use Apple iTunes to transfer the songs up the cable and onto the iPod? Somewhere around 2005 I was travelling on business to the USA a couple of times a year and, returning to the UK from one such trip to Atlanta, I decided to spoil my then teenage kids with a new iPod each. A couple of months later, one of the iPods developed a fault. Here we go, I thought. Getting a repair in the UK on equipment bought in the USA is going to be troublesome. I might even have to wait until I go back to the USA to get this sorted. I logged the fault, confirmed the iPod's serial number, and Apple instantly declared that a repair would be covered by warranty and that we would receive a refurbished device (same colour/specification) once they had received our faulty unit and diagnosed that it wasn't because of misuse or damage. At Apple's cost, UPS collected the unit from our home and a few days later a replacement unit arrived. Everything about the replacement unit oozed an impression of being brand new and for me set the benchmark for customer support with faulty items.

It now seemed to me that Microsoft hadn't researched how to deal with customers buying high-end products that fail because of an issue with the product itself, and not because of misuse or damage by the customer. That would be a whole different premise.   And there was to be no flexibility because my device was just outside the totally inflexible 'dead-on-arrival' period. Computer said no (theirs obviously, as mine wasn't working!), and the customer support operative hadn't got any empowerment to do anything other than that documented in the scripted process, however much they proclaimed their empathy and sympathy for my loss.

My old Lenovo laptop was still working, and I had my iPad that this Microsoft Surface Pro 4 was supposed to make obsolete for me. I now emailed customer support again and couldn't get any further than the standard response previously offered. Microsoft's computer system might say 'no', but Duncan didn't. My challenge was now to find someone in a senior position at Microsoft and appeal to their better judgement on providing a level of customer service befitting their professional product and MY cost of acquiring one.

It might have been quicker just to have put up a website detailing my dissatisfaction, but my websites have always been the weapon of 'last-resort,' even though trying to find the name and contact details for the person responsible, let alone ensuring a message got to them, would actually take longer than constructing and hosting a website.

Using LinkedIn, I found out the name of a Director at Microsoft who might take some responsibility. In her LinkedIn profile, the Chief Operating Officer (COO) for Microsoft in the UK states that she possesses a 'can-do' attitude. She was the person for me to contact, only how can you find an email address for anyone in a senior position at Microsoft? I couldn't. Companies like Microsoft actively protect contact details from being in the public domain, and even with my 'search engine skills' I couldn't find an email address for this person, nor could I find a common format for the few Microsoft employees in the UK that I was able to see an email address for. Instead, I picked up the phone and rang Microsoft's UK Headquarters in Reading and asked to be put through to her. I immediately discovered that this wasn't company policy, nor could I be put through to her PA. I explained to the operator, who I could sense was really trying their best to be helpful, why I wanted to contact the COO and she told me to send a message for the COO's attention via the email address for the switchboard at Microsoft that she gave me, and they would pass it on. Other than this, anything else was against company policy and not available to her or me as a remedy.

I wasn't hopeful. When I recently read back the email to Microsoft that I sent over four years ago, in February 2016, I'm a little surprised that it got any response. It was too long, too opinionated, but nonetheless it somehow worked. The COO didn't respond directly to me, but later that evening I received a phone call on my mobile from someone in customer services at Microsoft in the USA to whom my problem had been escalated to for them to solve. Juan was his name, and when he realised that he was dealing with someone who actually knew what they were doing with PC technology and who had exhausted all the suggested remedies, including a USB reboot to reimage the hard drive – which hadn't solved the problem – Juan provided a solution. Microsoft's computer system still said no to a DOA replacement, but as I had purchased my Surface Pro directly from the Microsoft store, he would now authorise a full refund on the basis that I re-purchased a replacement Surface Pro 4 first. I had to shell out another £1500 to buy my second Surface Pro 4, email Juan proof of my purchase, after which he sent me a pre-paid label to send the faulty unit back and which would trigger a refund back to my credit card once it had been safely received in Germany.

Finally, after many emails, conversations and having had the tenacity to contact Microsoft's COO in the UK (which shouldn't be necessary and which most people wouldn't have had the insight and determination to do) I had the outcome that I wanted. But here's the thing, here's the bit that I think companies like Microsoft who sell a premium product but don't have a premium customer service solution, are missing. I've never had any doubts about reliability with any of the many Apple products I have purchased since those first iPods, even though one failed. The way that Apple conducted their customer support was a truly great customer experience. Technically, for over four years now, my replacement Surface Pro 4 has been 100% reliable, but my perception is very different; I've never fully trusted my Surface Pro 4, and I know that's held me back from investing my time to fully adopt it as a replacement iPad – which it has never become for me. From a business point of view, all my documents are synced up to a cloud service, so I can't lose documents irretrievably. Four years on my Surface Pro 4 is ready to be replaced – possibly recycled to a family member – but it won't be replaced with a Microsoft purchase. If you're going to produce a premium product, you must live up to it.

I wanted to use this example with Microsoft, as a contrast to the examples with BMW, TUI and VW, to highlight a few different circumstances and also demonstrate that not every complaint has to be escalated to a protest website after the first setback.

What I'd say to Microsoft (and other large companies reading this)

- Find out how the customer wants their complaint resolved.
- As a consumer buying a product with his own money, I didn't want my expensive purchase devalued - in my eyes - with a refurbished device that presumably had already gone wrong for someone else.
- With a lower-priced purchase the expectation will probably be different – I was prepared to accept a re-furbished iPod because the value was less, the unit was already around 6 months old, and I was not the one directly using it. In a business situation, where the device is provided by an employer, having a refurbished unit might not be an issue, and the company might keep some 'spares' to recirculate in such scenarios.
- Crucially, empower your customer support staff to go 'off script' when required and fix problems in a human, personal way.

A premium product needs a premium customer service – not just a premium sales machine.

People judge brands by the way that they behave when things go wrong – this is your opportunity to differentiate, to stand out from the crowd. Turn problem solving into brand advocate creation.

When buying an item that would be classed as 'aspirational' and expensive compared to mainstream alternatives, then everything about that experience from pre-sales to the 'something's-gone-wrong service' must be supplied at the highest levels of quality and care. Some of us are prepared to pay for good service; indeed, I assumed I was!

So here was an example of fighting the machine to get to the right person who was empowered (or senior enough) to make a difference. This didn't need escalating to a protest website to get the desired outcome, but given that I would not have accepted a refurbished unit in this circumstance, if I hadn't gone the extra mile to get the resolution, I would probably have had a go at embarrassing Microsoft with one.

In summary, if you're going to produce a premium product, you must live up to it. That means the way you fix problems must be premium too. For me, based on my personal experiences, there is simply no comparison between Microsoft and Apple; Apple wins hands down every time.

Mastering Microsoft

- Find the right person. Leapfrog the script-restricted customer support teams and go to someone in a senior position and appeal to their better judgement. You will need to do some research here – what I call the 'Company Protection' Service kicks-in to prevent you getting your individual issue resolved.
- Contact that person directly either by telephone, email or letter. It helps if you can find out something that will resonate with them. In this case I saw on the executive's LinkedIn profile that she was a "Can Do" person. I directly told her that here was an opportunity to demonstrate that 'Can Do' attitude as well as pointing out that I didn't think Microsoft's policy on this premium product would satisfy the professional market.
- Be polite – never lose your temper, raise voice, etc.
- Show perspective – don't make greedy or unrealistic demands.
- Not every complaint has to be escalated to a protest website. Indeed, all the companies that I targeted with protest websites were given opportunities to provide a minimum level of acceptable customer service that would have made such action unnecessary.

Chapter Six

How to make sure that your Emails get read

There's no point creating a single-issue website to highlight your complaint if nobody reads it.

Whilst we could ensure some clever use of meta tags to help search engines list our website so that any member of the public searching for BMW, or TUI, etc. might serendipitously find it, we really want to make its existence actively known to people on the executive leadership team in the company causing our frustration. If the website's content is accurate and the truth portrays the company in a bad light, then someone in a leadership position, not working to a 'customer service script or process,' will have the necessary gravitas to initiate a resolution. Which is all we were after right from the start; a just settlement for the poor performance experienced.

A great email, crafted correctly and sent to the right people at the right time, will get your website read.

Why not a letter?

A letter, even with the added expense of a signed-for delivery, is very unlikely to reach the member of the senior leadership team it is addressed to. Social media and review sites such as TripAdvisor make it easy to register a complaint, so how do you stand out amongst the general noise that an increased volume of complaints generates? Complaints are handled by customer service, not the CEO, and so the CEO's secretary, who will open the letter, will scan it, identify a complaint, and send your best efforts to the customer service team without the CEO even being aware of it.

Executive Assistants, secretaries to C-Level executives, will also have a duplicate of the CEO's email's on their computer screens, and once again perform the role of first line of defence to keep anything away from the CEO that should ordinarily be dealt with by someone else. But, with a bit of nous, we can overcome this challenge and get the CEO to open the email.

And if we can get the CEO to open the email, a link will take them instantly to our website which, if they can read it, so can anyone else on the planet. A posted letter doesn't' have a clickable link and therefore the instant reinforcement in a single click provided by our email is absent. We are relying on them to put down the letter and type a web address into a browser.

Sunday Trading?

Executive Assistants, especially in the corporate world, do work long hours, but generally they don't work on a Sunday evening. And a Sunday evening is often a quiet time for a CEO to catch up on a bit of work, or to sit down in front of the TV with their work mobile phone within arm's reach. Waiting for a 'ding.'

An email coming into a CEO's inbox on a Sunday evening is therefore unlikely to be quickly snaffled away by an executive assistant. If the subject title is compelling enough to get the interest of a CEO, then most likely they will open it, even if they don't recognise the name of the sender and don't deem it to be a phishing scam.

How do I know this? It's worked for me several times, with TUI, with BMW, and even back in the day with VW when mobile email was in its infancy, only on a Blackberry™, and more likely to be read than today. Sunday has proven to be an effective tactic.

More's Law

The real Moore's Law is that the power of computer processing will roughly double every two years whilst the cost decreases 50%, but Duncan's "More's Law" is that copying more people from the senior leadership team can help your email be successful. Why? Because if you've copied other senior executives into the distribution of your email, the CEO is more likely to open and read it because they will assume that the others will and they won't want to be ignorant of what others are reading, especially if it's a Sunday evening and the wife's watching Vera. And so they'll open it and, if you've got your email perfectly crafted, they'll read it.

What about a Tuesday?

Now there's two interesting points here. Firstly, research suggests that a Tuesday morning after 10am is a good time for sending emails; any catch-up from the weekend or week before will have been completed by then. And secondly, in some circumstances Sunday will increasingly not be as good a strategy as it has historically proven to be. Why? As the focus on mental health and wellbeing rightly drives forwards, the 'always-on' organisational culture is being questioned like never before, and the constant availability outside of working hours with some expectations of out-of-hours responses, especially when working with colleagues in different time zones, is being robustly challenged. Some organisations in Germany have their email systems configured to hold any emails received after 6.15pm until the start of the next working day. In 2017, France introduced the El Khomri Law that requires employers to negotiate with employees about out-of-hours communications, and in the USA legislation is being proposed that will make it illegal for employers to insist that employees are contactable outside office hours by email.

The Perfect Email

How many times have we written an email, clicked send, and then almost immediately it's been sent, wish that we'd taken a bit more care? Or attached the attachment! Or even accidentally clicked on send when the email isn't finished?

For those of you that are technically very savvy and use Microsoft's Outlook to manage your emails, there's a way of putting a (short) delay as an instruction for all your emails, so that after you've clicked send, emails don't leave your Outbox for x number of minutes. This could be frustrating if you just want to immediately send a very short email to agree or disagree to something, but then perhaps you should be using Instant Messaging for that instead?

With an important email that I want to make sure is perfect, the first thing I do is take the urgency out of the equation. Under the 'Options' menu in Outlook, 'Delay Delivery' allows you to select a future date and time for when you want your email to send. The default is for 5pm on the day you create your email, but you can quickly change this to 7.30pm on Sunday.

I usually don't want to delay it by so long, but I leave the default at 5pm and then once I'm ready to hit send, I go back into 'Delay Delivery' and remove the instruction by unclicking the box.

Another option is to write your email without putting anyone in the 'To' address line, in which case it can't be sent until you are happy with your email and only then do you add the recipient(s).

Start with the End

What do you want your email to achieve? With my complaints, I wanted the recipient to click the link to see that my complaint was available on a website for anyone, anywhere to view, where the facts supporting my claims for poor goods or services were laid out with supporting pictures and videos for all to see.

To achieve this, the email must:

- Have a compelling 'Subject Line' that is personalised.
- Contain an immediate attention grabber that can't be ignored.
- Have a link that compels them to click and follow it.
- Convey the right tone, concisely and unambiguously (no waffle).

- Specify your call to action and let them assume that the consequence of inaction will be your website for all to read. This should not be stated as a threat, i.e. if you don't do this, I will do that. Your website is just documenting the nature of your complaint and the current unwillingness of the company to take any ownership of the situation.
- Be clear how to contact you.

Compelling Subject Line

Lies, damned lies, statistics and perhaps even urban myths, would have us believe that almost 80% of emails don't get opened and read. In these cases, the sender and subject title are enough to reach straight for the delete key or a left swipe on our phone screen.

When emailing the CEO of TUI in the UK (and copying senior colleagues in the UK and at the parent company in Germany), I used "The Broken Sensatori Promise" as my subject title. For VW, I used "Loyal VW Customer Threatened with Court Order" as the Subject line. Both achieved quick responses.

In these examples, Sensatori is one of TUI premium brands that implies great care and attention throughout your holiday, and for VW, what company would want a loyal customer to be threatened with a court order? In the email text, I very quickly established that I had previously purchased a number of VW's as private purchases and more recently chosen a VW from a range of options when selecting a company car.

Attention Grabber and link

Not only must the subject line do this, but the start of your email must continue to hold their interest. In essence, it's a brutal 'why this should be important to them' and what the consequence of creating a bad reputation might look like.

Don't start to explain your complaint in detail; you've already been down that road with the customer service team who have determined not to deal with your desire for acceptable recompense. If your website is named correctly, the link will lure them to read everything in detail.

For TUI, the click through to the website www.mySENSATORIexperience.co.uk worked perfectly, as did www.wouldYOUbuyaVWtiguan.co.uk with VW.

We want the reader to do more than just scan the first few lines and either delete or forward to someone else to deal with. We want them to instruct someone to get this sorted, because that means you are getting compensation for a justified complaint.

Do not attach a copy of your complaint. Many email systems will automatically block or quarantine an attachment from someone outside of their organisation which means that the message is unlikely to get through, especially if on Monday morning the Executive Assistant is in a position to intervene.

Convey the right tone

Without any waffle or ambiguity, anger or emotion, state clearly what you want the reader to do once they've accessed your website. Write it in such a way that if the email is forwarded on for someone else to action it, it can be done so without the CEO being caused any additional work to explain it.

What does success for you look like?

Now you have their attention, this is your chance to convince them that your complaint needs a resolution. If you know what you are looking for, state it clearly. With my complaint to TUI, I told them that I was looking for a refund equal to 50% of the cost. With BMW I told them that if they couldn't fix the problem, I wanted to return the car for a full refund. This is their call to action which in most cases will be the start of a proper negotiation to resolve the issue.

How to contact you

State again your email address at the end. If the email is forwarded on with the instruction to get the complaint resolved, the new person dealing with it won't now just be able to hit 'reply.'

Also provide a phone number as historically people won't simply agree to your view of what a settlement looks like, but will want to negotiate and this is a better experience by phone.

Don't send in haste

I return to my earlier point about not sending an email in haste, but instead to write, leave, edit, leave, and then send – sometimes the culture of immediacy makes us rush into sending when a review would make it more impactful. Allow time to make sure all the points that will provide a bigger effect can be incorporated. Taking time to properly craft your email will ensure better success.

Listen to your own words

Don't just proofread, as you can all too easily read in your head what you intended, but not what you've actually typed – i.e. you've typed 'than' instead of 'that,' but when you read it back you still read 'that.' So, use services like Microsoft's READ ALOUD, that is included with the latest versions of Word, Outlook, etc. Sit back and listen to someone else reading your words; I'm still surprised by the frequency with which the words that I've initially typed don't convey my original intention. So, listen and review, and make sure all opportunities for misinterpretation are eliminated.

Proof of email delivery

Another hidden gem in Outlook, again located within the 'Options' menu, are the opportunities to get acknowledgment that your email has been delivered, and that the recipient has opened the email and started to read the content. Organisational email is a complex business; different systems, different rules, some automate, some allow for manual selection by the recipient, etc. But be warned, even if you request a 'Read Receipt' it's entirely possible that someone has actually read your email but has declined the option to inform you.

Before you send your email, click on 'Options' and under the section called 'tracking' are two options to 'Request a Delivery Receipt' or 'Request a Read Receipt.' When your email arrives at the other end, if these acknowledgement requests are automatic, you will get a response. If it's a manual process, the recipient will get a dialogue box telling them that you've requested a 'delivery and / or read receipt,' and they have the option to send a receipt to you, or to decline your request.

Sometimes, finding an email address for the senior person you want can be difficult, but with some detective skills it's usually possible to either get confirmation or make an educated guess. So here are a few tips for...

Searching for a valid email address

Large organisations try to keep the contact details of their leadership teams out of the public domain, and they certainly don't promote them on their websites. Let's assume that you want to contact the CEO at Acme Corporation. It will be very easy to find their name; in the 'About Us' or 'News' section on their website, or just from a Google search for 'CEO Acme Corporation.' Bingo! We now know that the CEO is called Jayne Smith and the company's website is www.acme.com, so we do a search for a number of email formats of the name to see if it throws up a credible match; jayne.smith@acme.com, j.smith@acme.com, jsmith@acme.com. If none of these are confirmed, look on their website for any named contacts; these are most likely to be found in the Privacy Notice or Media Centre (where a directly named contact is often listed for Press Enquiries). You can then see if this person has an acme.com email address, or if for emails they use a different format. For example, some companies add 'mail' to the end of their web address just for emails. So instead it might be jayne.smith@acmemail.com.

If you're still struggling, there are some other places we can hunt. Firstly, find the corporate information section on their website and look in the 'Investor News' section or at the company's latest annual report. They are unlikely to state the CEO's contact details, but very often there will be a contact name and you get to see the email format they use. Another great resource for all sorts of information is Companies House. The amount of information available for free continues to surprise me, and many companies do their best to limit what is disclosed. You can also see if the CEO holds any other positions with other companies – sometimes their own consulting company – and if there are alternative contact details you can use.

If all these avenues fail, you can always take a best guess. If you send your email to jayne.smith@acme.com, the worst thing that can happen is that a few minutes later you get a 'bounce back' from the company's email server notifying you that the recipient is unknown. So now resend your email to j.smith@acme.com, and, if the same 'recipient unknown' response arrives, then jsmith@acme.com.

And finally, there's a really good resource for finding CEO email addresses at www.ceoemail.com. You might even start here if you don't want the fun and challenge of engaging in a little detective work!

Chapter Seven

Let's Build a Website and maybe embed a YouTube Video?

If you've decided, like me, that you're not getting the resolution that your complaint deserves and you now want to put up a website to make the facts known more widely, here's a guide to what's involved.

A website is going to take time and money, but how much of each depends on your digital skills and the time you have available, and whether you want to do this yourself or employ someone to create it for you. Unless your complaint is very complex, it could almost be an on-line accessible replicated version of your letters and emails, and quite simple and quick to achieve.

What precisely do you need?

1. A domain name that is ideally both self-descriptive and easy to remember.

For VW I used www.wouldyoubuyaVWtiguan.co.uk

For BMW I used www.myBMWexperience.co.uk and because I really wanted to annoy them,
I used the German translation of "My BMW Experience" and also put up a site at
www.meineBMWerfahrung.com

For TUI I used www.mySENSATORIexperience.co.uk as it was specifically their Sensatori brand that I was questioning.

And for The Chateau Impney, www.mychateauimpneyexperience.co.uk

2. A Web Hosting contract for your domain name. For people to find your website and for Search Engines such as Google to index it, your site

must be hosted by an ISP – Internet Service Provider – so that it's connected to the public internet for anyone to find and visit. There will be a charge for hosting – i.e. making your website publicly available to those that are looking for it.

My tactic was to make people associated with the company I was complaining about aware of the website. It can take time and money for services known as Search Engine Optimisation to promote your website to people just randomly searching for information connected with your website content.   To me, it wasn't important to draw other consumers in, but it was important to let people working in senior positions for the company I had my grievance with, to know that my site was publicly available.

3.	The content for your website that either you will design, or you will employ someone to do this on your behalf.

Where do you get Domain Names and Web Hosting from?

You need to commit to a contract with a provider such as wix.com, godaddy.com, 1&1 Ionos, who will sell you a webhosting contract and a domain name. Clearly you can't have the same domain name as one that has already been registered, and most providers have a Domain Name Checker feature on their website that allows you to check if it's already been taken. You can also just type the domain name into your search engine to also check availability.

These companies will state the minimum length of contract – usually at least six months and often twelve – usually as a monthly cost or with a discount for the first twelve months up front. I've always used 1&1 IONOS for my hosting, and the cost for the most basic package – which should be all you need for a site that is just providing information – is typically around £7 per month. Sometimes there are introductory offers of a reduced amount for three or six months, and sometimes an available Domain Name is included too. You need to check with a provider to find the exact costs, but at £7 per month with a minimum twelve-month contract, you are looking at a cash investment of £84 to register a Domain Name and host your site. But if the compensation you are seeking is considerable, £84 is almost identical to the cost of issuing a claim using the Money Claims Service of the HM Courts and Tribunal Service.

Web Hosting plans

Each hosting provider will offer a range of plans; the more you pay the more features the service will offer you. This will include things like the number of email accounts you have with your website. You will probably need just one – I'd recommend having an email address separate to your usual email. For example, I had duncan@mybmwexperience.co.uk and set this up so that it would automatically forward to my usual email address. Another variation is the number of websites you can have for your hosting and the amount of space on their server. These larger facilities are designed for companies who will have many employees (so lots of email addresses required), and will put lots of information on their website; organisational structure, products, support, customer service, etc. And if you want to have a shop that allows people to buy multiple items and take payments, you will need additional facilities too. For a simple website that will just host the information on one or two pages, the basic will more than do.

Designing a Website

There are three ways to do this.

1. Buy webhosting that includes the software and templates for creating your website content. This is typically known as a 'Sitebuilder' or 'Web-builder' service or similar.

    When you log into your account, the designs you create will automatically be associated with your domain name.

2. Use 3rd party software to design your website.

   Your hosting provider will provide you with a link to the space on their server for your domain name, and when your design is completed, you upload the file(s) to the server using the username and password supplied. This is known as FTP; File Transfer Protocol, and many web design software packages include it. There are free-of-cost FTP packages if they don't.

3. Pay someone to create and upload your website for you. For a single page website, I would like to think that it should be no more than £150. This is assuming that you have supplied them the words and pictures by email, and they just have to make it look pretty and ensure that the links to any additional pages or external content are working.

Hold the FrontPage!

One of the reasons that I devised the single-issue website to escalate my complaints, was the fact that I already had some basic web design skills and knew how to host a website. As a side-line to my full-time job, over 20 years ago I started writing small websites, mainly for owners of independent Bed & Breakfast businesses, who wanted to advertise their business on-line. At that time Microsoft had a great product called FrontPage. Whilst the early websites were all developed with using raw programming code, FrontPage enabled you to set out text and images on a page – in a similar way to their word processor (Word™) and desktop publishing (Publisher™) tools – and simply upload this to a web host.

FrontPage was discontinued or replaced with something else, and for many years I've used a package called Designer Pro from a company called Xara, which can be purchased at www.magix.com.

To help me, I already had the experience of registering domain names, contracting webspace, and the skills to create content and upload it. Creating my websites were the proverbial 'no brainer.'

There are other issues associated with websites, especially if you are trying to promote them to customers who don't know you exist, so that they come up in web searches, etc. But for me I was just going to target as many people as possible associated with the company I was complaining against, so this wasn't an important factor or required any additional investment. There is an industry all of its own for optimising website for search engine success, and the charges can be quite high. But then if you are selling expensive goods and services, those charges are all part of your marketing spend.

Most websites are part of a marketing strategy that will be built over many years, where my aim is to have the website hosted for as short a period of time as necessary. In the instance with The Chateau Impney, this was just a couple of hours, whereas the site hosting my BMW experience has been live for over four years and continues to typically attract 100 visitors per week. My internet service provider (ISP), 1and1 Ionos, sends an automated weekly report and for the period 06/04/2020 to 12/04/2020 they reported 42 visitors to the German site (www.meinebmwerfahrung.com) and 63 visitors to the UK site (www.mybmwexperience.co.uk). My YouTube video, showing the BMW DAB radio losing reception whilst the inexpensive PURE portable DAB radio continues to play, has now had 8342 views (as at 14/07/2020).

Feedback from other complainants

There is every likelihood that other people will have had their own grievances with the organisation you are complaining about, and they will find your website – especially if it is hosted for enough time to automatically register with search engines and you have included tags to reference it to what people might be looking for.

Do you want people to contact you or just read your story? If you want some supporting comments, then you can either just use an email address (i.e. duncan@mychateauimpneyexperience.co.uk) which you can ask your ISP to forward to your regular email address, or you can incorporate a feedback form into your website – this will be one of the features of the site you need to subscribe to if it's important to you.

WordPress

WordPress – www.wordpress.com – has become a dominant player for creating websites, especially those that incorporate blogs and other regular updates. I have never used them but given their dominance and the simplicity that many people tell me they offer, if I was looking to create a website for the first time, I'd definitely check them out. They also offer paid-for packages for hosting, but the actual WordPress software is free. Other hosting companies increasing support WordPress as the web building platform, with 1&1 IONOS having a dedicated WordPress hosting service that keeps the software updated without any intervention from you.

Inserting a Video

We are all used to capturing video on our smartphones and tablets then sharing them with family and friends using applications such as WhatsApp, Instagram, Facebook, etc.

In the case of my video that shows an inexpensive portable DAB radio outperforming the DAB installed in my BMW, I just filmed it using an iPhone and uploaded it directly to YouTube – having first created a YouTube account. There wasn't any editing of the video involved, as the evidence I was aiming to capture occurred after just two minutes in and in fact this lead in built up the expectation of what was to come. Unless they have a specific interest, generally people will not watch a video clip that is longer than a couple of minutes, in many cases much less.

If you do want to edit your video and add captions there's lots of free editing software out there, including Apple's own iMovie.

YouTube allows you to embed the video into your website, or you can create a link from the website to open it in YouTube. You can also allow people viewing your video to leave comments.

There's little point me adding much more at this stage. The website companies that I've mentioned will all directly or indirectly support video and the instructions will vary depending on which system you use. I'm sure that they'll have their own video help files with clear instructions that you can watch and there are plenty of video instruction videos on YouTube; I know because I've watched a few and quickly realised that these resources are much better than anything I can offer here in word form.

Finally, Good Luck

If you do decide to follow my example and create a website to promote your frustrations far and wide, then good luck and I hope you get the outcomes you require. For me it wasn't about the money, it was about standing up to big corporations who have massive resources to fight legal actions, and who make many people give up by continually fobbing them off with standard letters that don't deal with your situation properly.

Keep Calm and Carry On Complaining

Acknowledgements

This book might not have happened without the encouragement and support of Lucy Green who not only encouraged me to write up my experiences, but generously provided feedback and great advice.

I met Lucy by chance when we rented one of her fabulous thatched cottages located in the shadow of St. Michael's Church in Minehead's Higher Town. An oasis of calm that we have revisited many times.

Dog friendly with hot tubs and log burners, check out Lucy's website at

https://www.exmoorcharactercottages.co.uk/

I am grateful also to Joe Purnell of 1935 Design for creating the cover.

If you need a website, business cards or a snazzy new logo, Joe's your man. www.nineteenthirtyfive.co.uk

And to the following dear friends and family, I am also indebted for providing a combination of proof reading, sense checking, literary advice, and general encouragement:

Jan Davies

Sophie James

Mandy Nunnington

Daphne O'Brien

.

Whilst You're Here......

If you have enjoyed reading this book, why not challenge yourself to work out 'whodunit'?

Youthenasia – by Duncan Peberdy

As well as being a page-turning read incorporating dark thoughts and desperate deeds, Youthenasia is also the ultimate 1980's pop-music quiz.

Expertly crafted into the text are the song titles from 85 Top 20 UK hit singles from the 1980s*. Songs by top-selling artists such as George Michael, Duran Duran, Tears for Fears, Depeche Mode, Iron Maiden, Michael Jackson, Bruce Springsteen, David Bowie and many more.

Available on Kindle from Amazon for just £2.99[#]

Image © Neil Duffy

*As listed in the Guinness book "Hits of the 80s."
[#]Price correct at time of going to press.